Cloze Procedure and the Teaching of Reading

James Rye

Head of English,
St. Clement's High School,
King's Lynn

HEINEMANN EDUCATIONAL BOOKS
LONDON and EXETER (NH)

Heinemann Educational Books Ltd
22 Bedford Square, London WC1B 3HH

Heinemann Educational Books Inc
4 Front Street, Exeter, New Hampshire 03833

LONDON EDINBURGH MELBOURNE AUCKLAND
HONG KONG SINGAPORE KUALA LUMPUR NEW DELHI
IBADAN NAIROBI JOHANNESBURG EXETER (NH)
KINGSTON PORT OF SPAIN

First published 1982

British Library Cataloguing in Publication Data

Rye, James
    Cloze procedure and the teaching of reading.
    1. Reading – Study and teaching
    2. Cloze procedure
    I. Title
    428.4′07′1   LB1050

    ISBN 0-435-10781-X

Typeset by Inforum Ltd, Portsmouth
Printed in Great Britain by
Biddles Ltd, Guildford and King's Lynn

Contents

List of Figures   *iv*

List of Tables   *iv*

Preface   *v*

Acknowledgements   *vii*

1 Cloze Procedure and Reading   *1*

2 Measuring Readability   *12*

3 Measuring Reading Ability   *29*

4 Developing Reading Ability   *47*

5 Some Factors in Passage Preparation   *58*

6 Towards Diagnosis and Possible Remedies   *73*

7 Cloze Across the Curriculum   *88*

Appendix   *101*

Glossary   *105*

Bibliography   *111*

Index   *119*

List of Figures

Fig. I   – Sampling, Constructing, Matching
Fig. II   – Factors in Readability
Fig. III   – Percentage Cloze Scores
Fig. IV   – Cloze Readability Scores for Different Bible Versions
Fig. V   – The Difficulty of Prediction of Different Word Classes
Fig. VI   – The Frequency of Different Word Classes
Fig. VII   – Position in Sentence and Difficulty of Prediction
Fig. VIII   – Relationship Between Length of Unilateral Context (in Letters) and Constraint
Fig. IX   – Relationship Between Length of Bilateral Context (in Words) and Constraint
Fig. X   – Summary of Factors Affecting Difficulty of Prediction
Fig. XI   – The Percentage of Variance in Taylor's Comprehension Test that can be Predicted by the Cloze Test

List of Tables

Table I   – Cloze Readability Scores
Table II   – Criterion Scores for Cloze Readability Tests
Table III   – Some Tests involving Types of Cloze Procedure
Table IV   – Validity Coefficients for *The Day It Rained*
Table V   – Readability Coefficients for *The Day It Rained*
Table VI   – First Stage Analysis of Cloze Errors
Table VII   – Mean Scores on Cloze and Comprehension Tests
Table VIII   – Correlation Between Scores on the Cloze and Comprehension Tests

Preface

Of all the activities considered as aids to reading development by the Schools Council *Reading for Learning* Project based at Nottingham University, Cloze Procedure is the one which has the largest number of research studies associated with it. Ever since Wilson Taylor invented the practice in 1953, studies have been carried out which have either sought to shed light on Cloze Procedure itself, or which have used it as a tool for understanding what takes place when an individual reads a text. Considering the volume of specialist literature available, it is perhaps strange that Cloze Procedure has taken so long to become moderately popular. Christopher Walker's book, *Reading Development and Extension*, the Bullock Report, *A Language for Life*, and the Schools Council Project reports, *The Effective Use of Reading* and *Extending Beginning Reading* have undoubtedly helped the practice move from the realms of psycholinguistic research to the everyday realities of the classroom.

As Cloze Procedure becomes more popular the need to fully understand its strengths and weaknesses becomes more urgent. During the past few years I have attended several in-service courses for teachers which have recommended using Cloze Procedure in the classroom. At only one of these courses was any meaningful attempt made to look at the practical difficulties of ensuring that the Procedure is effective, and none of them offered any serious indication of the full range of uses that cloze has. This book was written as an attempt ot meet these two needs.

In the area of developing comprehension, the Bullock Report has argued that the mere filling in of gaps as a routine exercise is of doubtful educational value. Unless one understands what factors contribute to meaningful gap filling, and how these factors can be encouraged and managed in the classroom, there is a real danger that the Procedure will be a pointless exercise. I have tried to suggest ways of developing good, professional classroom practices with cloze in a variety of areas.

Unlike many activities associated with reading, Cloze Procedure has a wide range of applications. It is this versatility which is one of the factors which makes it so useful to the teacher. To learn about Cloze Procedure can be to learn something about each of the following: the psychology of the reading process; the measurement of readability;

the development of reading; the diagnosis of reading failure; the testing of subject knowledge; and reading for learning in the subject areas. As well as suggesting a variety of ideas for use in the classroom it is hoped that this book will provide the reader with some understanding of a whole range of topics connected with the teaching of reading. Each of these topics is usually treated separately in the literature. This book draws them together in a single volume.

Chapter One is an explanation of what Cloze Procedure is. I have tried to show the similarities and differences between Cloze Procedure and the normal reading process. Although this chapter is mainly theoretical, the explanation of cloze which it provides underlies many of the assumptions and arguments which are made in the remainder of the book.

Chapters Two and Three consider how the interaction between the reader and the cloze passage can be used to gauge the readability of books and the reading ability of the child. These chapters are not intended to be an exhaustive treatment of readability and testing in general. However, they do indicate the advantages cloze passages have over some assessment methods and instruments. They also give clear indications as to how the teacher can use Cloze Procedure in these areas. Particular attention is paid to the factors which have to be borne in mind when interpreting results.

Chapters Four and Five take a closer look at the notion of Cloze Procedure as a means of developing reading. What, precisely, can cloze do to help reading? Although part of the answer is informed spectulation, Chapter Four illustrates the potential of cloze, and both chapters suggest ways of making cloze effective. Chapter Five concentrates on factors which determine the difficulty of deletions.

The final two chapters return to the three main themes of the earlier part of the book, namely of using cloze as a means of understanding reading, as a means of testing, and as a means of developing reading. They explore these in greater detail by looking at specific reading problems that cloze can reveal, and at how the Procedure can be used to help teachers in a variety of subject areas.

The aim of this book is not to encourage teachers to give children meaningless exercises to complete: it is to help teachers use Cloze Procedure to understand more about the reading behaviour of their children, and to help them assist their children in making reading progress.

Wherever possible I have avoided technical terms, but in certain aspects of the subject, especially where measurement is involved, some use has to be made of statistical terminology. The reader unfamiliar with terms such as *mean* and *correlation coefficient* is referred to the Glossary.

Acknowledgements

My first acknowledgement, appropriately, is to the inventor of Cloze Procedure, Wilson L. Taylor, and to the American Psychological Association, for permission to reproduce in adapted form in Tables VII and VIII copyright material from his article 'Cloze readability scores as indices of individual differences in comprehension and aptitude' in the *Journal of Applied Psychology*, 41 (1), pp. 19–26, 1957. I am grateful also to my present publishers and the authors of the *GAP* and *GAPADOL* reading tests, John McLeod and John Anderson, for allowing me to include extracts; to John McLeod for much helpful background information; and to John Bormuth for kindly agreeing to the reproduction of Table II.

I am indebted to the Editors of the *Evangelical Times* for allowing me to reproduce my figures on the readability of the *Bible*; to Thomas Nelson and Sons for permission to use part of the *Wide-span Reading Test*; to N.F.E.R.-Nelson for permission to use part of the *London Reading Test*; to Oliver and Boyd for permission to use part of the *Schonell Silent Reading Test B*; to the Editors of *English in Education* for allowing me to reproduce one of my transcripts in Chapter Four which first appeared in their journal, and to the Editors of *Language For Learning* who gave first publication to a slightly different version of the section on 'Training' which appears in the same chapter; to the Longman Group for permission to adapt passages from two of their textbooks for illustrative purposes in Chapter Seven.

Various friends and colleagues have given encouragement and helped in the development of this book. David Brentnall and Neil Batcock have given their assistance in helping obtain elusive reference material, and Victor Carter and Margaret Raines of the Norfolk Remedial Advisory Service have loaned from their professional libraries. I am also grateful to Pearl Sjölander for her help in the development of 'The Day It Rained'.

My greatest debt is to my wife, Nina, whose patience and skill have been continually drawn upon, and to the children I have taught who have helped me to learn about Cloze Procedure.

Chapter One

Cloze Procedure and Reading

What is Cloze Procedure?

Cloze Procedure is not the mystifying psychological technique that perhaps the name suggests. Neither is it simply a process of requiring readers to fill gaps in sentences. The Bullock Report (D.E.S. 1975) described Cloze Procedure as 'the use of a piece of writing in which certain words have been deleted and the pupil has to make maximum possible use of context clues available in predicting the missing words'. (p. 93)

The way the reader goes about filling in the gaps is all-important. The use of the surrounding context to help the reader guess the missing word is essential to the concept of Cloze Procedure as a meaningful way of helping reading in the classroom.

Before looking at the process in detail, what takes place during the cloze process can be briefly illustrated in the following example. Read the passage below and supply the one word which you think is missing from the gap.

> The professional development of teachers is something which is sadly neglected by some employing local authorities. This has been particularly true recently when financial assistance to help teachers go on courses has not been too forthcoming because of cutbacks in expenditure. The method of paying teachers additional increments up to a certain level seems to assume a degree of professional improvement. All too often this development is allowed to happen by chance.
>
> This situation is ————, particularly when one considers the potential enrichment that is being kept from pupils as well as from their teachers.

The surrounding context informs the reader that the writer is not content with the situation, and the grammatical construction requires an adjective. Already the context has been used to eliminate thousands of possibilities. Unless the 'answer' is provided, as it will not be in this case, we can never know for certain what the 'right answer' is.

However, the reader may have reasoned something like this:

> 'Unfortunate' is a possibility. It would fit in with the tone of 'sadly' used in the first sentence. The feeling in the passage would perhaps suggest something stronger than 'unfortunate'. The phrase 'particularly when' following the deletion adds weight to the strength of feeling against the situation. 'Unfortunate' is too weak, 'disgusting' is perhaps too strong; 'scandalous' would be a successful compromise.

Why 'Cloze' Procedure?

The human mind has a tendency to complete incomplete patterns or sequences. In the diagram below the reader's mind could easily supply the missing segments, enabling him or her to see a circle.

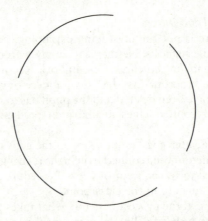

When Cloze Procedure was first reported as being a potentially useful practice in 1953, Taylor explained it in terms of this ability which the mind has to complete patterns. He thought of Cloze Procedure as a means of measurement and wrote about the 'cloze unit' (that is, the deleted word) as follows:

> At the heart of the procedure is a functional unit of measurement tentatively dubbed a 'cloze'. It is pronounced like the verb 'close' and is derived from 'closure'. The last term is one gestalt psychology applies to the human tendency to complete a familiar but not-quite-finished pattern – to 'see' a broken circle as a whole, for example, by mentally closing up the gaps. . . . One can complete the broken circle because its shape or pattern is so familiar that, although much of it is actually missing, it can be recognised anyway.
>
> The same principle applies to language. . . .

This theoretical model for Cloze Procedure based on gestalt psychology has been popular but it has serious weaknesses. This model may describe what happens in some cases of *perception*, but filling in cloze deletions is not about 'seeing' patterns in the sense of seeing the pattern of a circle. Cloze Procedure is essentially a *cognitive* task. The reader has to reason and construct suggestions to fill the gap on the basis of the evidence derived from the context. It is true that there are grammatical 'patterns' in language. The reader's innate ability to produce grammatically appropriate sentences will help determine the grammatical class of the word to be produced. However, the completion of meaning, based on understanding and reasoning, is a cognitive task. Ohnmacht et al (1970) concluded that there was no strong relationship between the gestalt principle of closure, and the completion of items in a cloze passage. Although it is too late to change the name I hope to show in the remainder of this chapter that 'Construction Procedure' may be a more accurate title for the process.

Before looking in greater detail at what takes place when a person completes a cloze deletion it will be helpful to understand something of what takes place when a fluent reader reads a passage without deletions.

Fluent Reading – a 'Guessing Game'.
Writing involves the physical formation of individual letters which in turn become words. It is tempting to think that reading simply involves the processing of individual bits of graphic information and then the putting of these individual bits together. However, reading is more than the sum of a sequence of individual letter and word perceptions. When reading, the mind is not merely a mainly passive receptacle that is filled with graphic information simply for the purpose of identification.

There is considerable evidence to support this view of reading. Much of that evidence has been reported by Ryan and Semmel (1969) and it will be helpful to repeat some of it here.

Experiments using a tachistoscope (an instrument which will display an image for a determined amount of time) have shown that some words can be recognised faster than letters. This would not be possible if the reading process involved decoding each letter in a word. If this were the case one would expect the time taken to recognize a word to be equal to the sum of the individual letter times. People also often claimed that they saw letters that were not present in the stimulus presented by the tachistoscope. For example, if 'foyever' was presented many people were convinced that they had seen 'forever'. Partial information gleaned from the stimulus word led them to *predict* that it would be spelt in a particular way, in spite of graphic evidence to the contrary. The eye seems to sample only part of the available information and then predict the rest.

Further evidence that each letter is not 'read' has been obtained from studies of how the eye behaves during reading. These have shown that the eye does not stop and focus on every letter. If this were the case the reader would be involved in making a large number of fixations for each line of print.

The fluent reader makes few fixations per line.

5   10   15   20   25   30   35

The fluent reader fixates, taking in several letters at a time, before jumping a number of letters and fixating again.

The fluent reader makes few fixations per line.

1   2   3

Systematic, successive, adjacent fixations are extremely difficult to sustain and would slow the reading process down immensely. The reader can prove this to himself by trying to consciously register every letter on this page.

Individual letters are not unrelated when presented in words. When used in meaningful language they frequently occur in certain sequences. The fluent reader knows this and is able to predict what is likely to follow on the basis of only a few letters. Unless one comes across relatively unfamiliar words like 'sciamachy', or 'solidungulate', all the graphic information given is not needed. Even here, most readers will pick out some familiar looking sequences (such as 'sci' or 'solid') rather than pausing at every single letter.

There is also evidence to show that sentences are not just the sum total of individual word perceptions. The eye does not focus on every letter when reading, neither does it always focus on every word. There are influences on words which help the reader predict what may be coming in a given sequence. This can be illustrated by the fact that children can sometimes recognize words when they are presented in the context of a sentence which remain unrecognized when presented in isolation. The fact that there are constraints operating between words can be further illustrated by sentences which contain the word 'read'. Look carefully at the following sentences:

The pupil wanted to read the book.
The teacher put the book down after she had read the story.

In both instances the graphic information from the letters 'read' is identical. It is the mind's appreciation of influences outside the individual word that determines how this graphic information is pronounced in each case. Ryan and Semmel also quote a study where subjects were asked to read passages that contained some grammatical errors. In a high proportion of cases these fluent readers corrected the errors and read them as if they did not exist. The readers appeared to be *more sensitive* to the grammatical relations of what they were reading than they were to the printed words themselves.

This kind of evidence has led psycholinguists and psychologists to reject the idea that the reading process simply involves the recognition of graphic information. Reading has been described as 'a psycholinguistic guessing game' (Goodman 1967), and 'a constructive language process' (Ryan and Semmel 1969). What the writers mean by this is that the fluent reader is able to use the factors in language which make letters and words predictable to construct hypotheses about what may be coming next in any language sequence. These hypotheses are then confirmed or modified as the eyes scan the ensuing context information. Not all the graphic information is needed. Perhaps the shape of the word or the first few letters are all that is needed to give some indication of what may be following and may be sufficient to confirm a previous hypothesis. In thinking without a book the mind constructs language by itself. When thinking with a book, the mind constructs language according to cues given by the book. In both the following quotations the italics are mine.

> Reading . . . [is] *externally guided thought* in which the stimulus, rather than determining perception, serves as a *prompter* for *ongoing language process*. (Neisser 1967)

> Reading is a process of *sampling* possible cues in the printed message, *constructing* a probable message and then *matching* it to the given output. (Goodman 1967)

Constraint on Words

There are various constraints which will enable the fluent reader to predict what may come next in any given language sequence. The reader uses his innate sense of what is grammatical and what is ungrammatical, his understanding of word meanings and his previous experience of words occurring together in a certain order.

Grammatical Constraints He got up ———— walked out.

Although grammatical constraint may not always be as clear as it is in the above sentence, the sentence does illustrate the importance that it can have. The construction requires a conjunction. Any other type of word would be totally inappropriate. It is not claimed that grammatical constraint will supply the answer but it is helpful in ruling out a large number of alternatives. The reader still has to decide on which particular conjunction to use, but the field which he has to choose from has now been considerably reduced.

Semantic Constraints As we walked home the moon was ———— .

If, for the purpose of this illustration, we assume that the missing word is a verb rather than an adjective, we could say that the sentence requires a verb that would convey a state or action usually associated with the moon. 'Screaming' would be completely unsuitable unless the sentence was describing part of a dream, a piece of science-fiction, or unless the word was being used in a figurative sense. In any of the above situations the sentence would require more than normally close reading because of the possibility of unexpected words. In a more usual context one would expect a verb such as 'shining'. The context helps to determine that certain words are unsuitable and makes others highly probable.

Coefficient of Usage There are some words which frequently occur in conjunction with other words. This is partly due to the constraints of grammar and meaning, but as Webster (1977) has pointed out, there are other factors which could account for the relatively high usage of certain phrases, and hence the relative ease of predicting any part of their sequence which may have been deleted. Previous experiences of reading or listening to these sequences enables the mind to remember them easily. Groups of words which have a high coefficient of usage may be considered as belonging to one or more of the following categories.

Collocation (Cup and saucer. Up and down.)
Rhythmic (Once upon a time.)
Alliterative Reinforcement (*St*and *st*ill. I *w*ent for a *w*alk.)
Assonantal Reinforcement (Wh*i*te l*i*e. Bl*a*ck m*a*gic.)

In any reading situation the different effects from particular constraints obviously overlap and usually operate on the reader at a subconscious level. However, without these factors which help the fluent reader anticipate what is coming next, reading would be an extremely laborious and slow process.

Cloze Procedure – Sampling, Constructing and Matching
It should be reasonably clear by now that the processes involved in fluent reading are in some ways similar to the processes involved in completing cloze deletions. It is precisely because of these similarities that it is claimed that Cloze Procedure may be one way of developing certain reading skills. This will be discussed further in Chapter Four.

When completing a cloze deletion the reader samples the context information, constructs a response and then checks this response with the available context information. If the reader thinks back to the example of Cloze Procedure given at the start of this chapter, syntactic and semantic clues were found in the context and used to produce words such as 'unfortunate', 'sadly', 'disgusting' and 'scandalous'. When these alternatives were matched or checked with the context, further information was found which suggested that most of them would be inappropriate. All the information available was used to select the most appropriate response.

In spite of the similarities it should be noted that there are important differences between Cloze Procedure and the normal reading process (See Fig. I). In normal reading the reader samples graphic information mainly from the context of the immediate sentence. When there is a problem of identification or of meaning that cannot be solved easily the eyes will move backwards and forwards, sometimes outside the

Figure I: Sampling, Constructing, Matching

	Normal Reading	*Cloze Procedure*
Sampling	Mainly sampling from within the sentence, following the word order of the sentence.	Within-sentence sampling, but also searching from a wider context.
Constructing	Subconcious construction based on previous experience of language, understanding of meaning and innate sense of grammar.	As with normal reading, but also conscious construction on the basis of a wider range of linguistic clues. An overt awareness of syntax and meaning is encouraged.
Matching	Matching predictions with specific graphic information.	Graphic clues cannot be directly matched with the anticipated word. Matching is done mainly on the basis of meaning.

immediate sentence, in search of information that will help. The fluent reader's eyes may also jump backwards occasionally in order to review what has been read. The cloze task makes this searching outside the immediate sentence even more necessary and more frequent. In cloze procedure the normal flow of the reading process is interrupted. If pupils are to become proficient in cloze they must consciously learn to search a wider context.

When constructing a response to fill a cloze deletion the reader will again tend to do this on a more conscious level than would an ordinary reader when anticipating the next word. In a group situation the reasons for the particular choice of word can be stated and discussed. The child who does not see the need to think through the reasons for the choice of a particular word and who does not become reasonably proficient in doing so is unlikely to have success with difficult deletions.

One further difference between fluent reading and Cloze Procedure lies in the area of matching. In fluent reading the reader is concerned with matching an anticipated word with a specific set of symbols. In Cloze Procedure there are no specific graphic clues to confirm the hypothesis. Although grammatical clues will help to some extent, the hypothesis stands or falls mainly on the strength of the match between the anticipated word and the reader's appreciation of semantic clues in the passage. If the anticipated word is 'wrong' this will be essentially due to a mis-match between the word and the *meaning* of the passage.

Other Procedures

In the literature on Cloze Procedure there are examples of practices which require different processes from the ones outlined above. They have various applications and some of them are outlined below for the purpose of discussing their different emphases. In general they are very limited in the educational opportunities they offer.

Selection from a List Some textbooks contain items like the following: Use one of the listed nouns to complete each of the sentences below.

> glazier
> policeman
> pharmacist
> chauffeur

1. A ——— earns his living by preparing and selling medicines.
2. A ——— earns his by preventing and detecting crime.
3. A ——— earns his by cleaning and driving a car.
4. A ——— earns his by fitting windows with glass.

Use one of the nouns to complete each of the sentences below.

>   sapling
>   gosling
>   cygnet

1. A young swan is called a ——— .
2. A young tree is referred to as a ——— .
3. A young goose is known as a ——— .

Usually this kind of exercise is found in books intended for primary pupils or for less able secondary pupils.

As with ordinary Cloze Procedure, there is a gap to be filled, but in this case the attention is more likely to be placed on the list of alternatives provided than on the context. Context clues, notably semantic ones, will play a small part if the correct word is to be selected, but the context no longer serves as a basis on which to construct possibilities. The possibilities are already provided and merely have to be checked out against the context. Also by limiting the context to one sentence the pupil is not being encouraged to develop the ability to search for important context clues which may lie outside the immediate sentence. The above exercises may encourage the pupil to think briefly about the meaning of a particular word from the list, but it is not likely to encourage him to generate language based on his appreciation of a passage. Nor are they likely to demand much thought about meaning. If pupils already know the word from the list it will not take long to fill the gap. If they do not know the word it may be possible to deduce it by a simple process of elimination in some cases. The context is not going to help them choose an unfamiliar word.

The focusing of attention on particular words or phrases which this practice requires can be usefully exploited and this kind of Cloze Procedure is not necessarily pointless. Marigold (1980) has reported ways of using this type of exercise as a means of drawing attention to dramatic language in poetry. Small groups of pupils are presented with a poem which has had certain phrases removed. These are listed below and the pupils are required to discuss which phrases they feel the poet would have used where, and why. The following short example is taken from the poem 'Electric Love' by Denis Glover.

'My love is like a ———
With woven ——— for hair,
And when she ——— it at night
The ——— run crackling there.

Oh, she is the ——— . . .'

wire, magnetic field, brushes, woven, sparks, dynamo

Again the process of elimination may help the pupil but this can be avoided if a large number of possibilities is given. When successful this practice can help draw attention to the meanings of particular words and phrases which might otherwise be glossed over. It could lead to discussions about what the poet was trying to achieve and hence lead to a deeper appreciation of the poem.

This practice is also useful in revising words which are specific to certain subjects. The use of Cloze Procedure in the subject areas will be discussed in Chapter Seven.

Additional Visual Clues Apart from supplying words at the end of the passage to choose from there are other more subtle ways of helping the pupil supply the missing word. Various types of visual clues can be given in addition to the linguistic clues already supplied by the context (Walker (1974)). The advantage of supplying visual clues as opposed to whole words is that the extent of the clue can be controlled by the teacher to suit the ability or experience in Cloze Procedure of the pupils concerned. The teacher can give enough information to help, without giving the whole answer away. The onus is still placed on the pupil to some extent to construct the missing word. These clues are important not only for young or poor readers who may be otherwise daunted by the cloze task, but also for capable readers when they start Cloze Procedure. The extra clues are one way of ensuring success in the early stages and of helping to establish the idea that each gap has just one word missing.

Additional information can be given concerning the initial letter or letters of the word, the length of the word and the word shape. Initial letters are perhaps the most useful as they set up expectations in the reader's mind about what may follow. Word shape is also important because, apart from indicating the number of letters in the word, it may give information about certain sequences of letters in that word. For example, the shape ⬜⬜ as part of a word strongly suggests the letters . . . ight.

Look carefully at the following passage and note how the amount of visual information given affects the ease of prediction of the missing words.

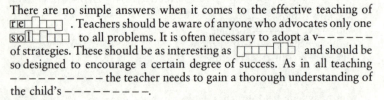

There are no simple answers when it comes to the effective teaching of re⬜⬜⬜⬜ . Teachers should be aware of anyone who advocates only one so⬜⬜⬜⬜ to all problems. It is often necessary to adopt a v— — — — — of strategies. These should be as interesting as ⬜⬜⬜⬜⬜⬜ and should be so designed to encourage a certain degree of success. As in all teaching — — — — — — — — — the teacher needs to gain a thorough understanding of the child's — — — — — — — —.

Although supplying visual clues has its place in the introduction of Cloze Procedure it is best to wean pupils off this practice as soon as they begin to experience success with it. The attention is still largely concentrated on the visual clue, rather than on the syntactic and semantic clues supplied in the context.

Summary
Cloze Procedure derived its title from the description of certain aspects of perception given by gestalt psychologists. Although extremely popular as a theoretical model such a view fails to take account of the cognitive nature of the cloze task.

The fluent reader is able to anticipate what is coming next in a language sequence on the basis of clues in the text. The processes involved in fluent reading are similar, in some respects, to those required in the completion of cloze deletions. Both activities involve the sampling of information from the context followed by the formation of, and checking of hypotheses. However, Cloze Procedure is a more conscious activity requiring a different kind of sampling and matching.

Whilst the practices of supplying alternative answers and of giving additional visual clues have their value in certain contexts, all such practices tend to limit the demands made on the pupils. They tend to draw attention away from the context.

Chapter Two

Measuring Readability

The Need for Assessment

'Assess, don't guess!' has become a popular slogan among those who wish to promote the intelligent use of reading tests. It has long been recognized that if meaningful, professional judgements are to be made, either when evaluating a course of instruction, or when assessing the progress of an individual pupil, some form of measuring instrument is required. Whilst the advantages and disadvantages of using these tests is not the main concern of this chapter, it needs to be borne in mind that, at best, these instruments provide only part of the information that is of possible interest to the teacher. Unless some measuring instrument can be applied to the reading material itself, the information about the child's reading ability is of limited value. It is one thing to know that according to a particular reading test a child may have a notional reading age of 9.6 years, but unless one can assess the readability level of the language that one wishes to give the child to read, the child may still receive language to read which is of inappropriate difficulty. If the language is too difficult the task will lead to frustration and an increasing lack of confidence about reading. If the child is continually given language which is too easy, the ability to accommodate increasingly complex language is not developed. Any means of assessing the language to be presented to children would be extremely valuable in helping make a happy match between language and their reading ability.

Most teachers of remedial pupils have been concerned for some time with assessing the language they present, and a few publishers now regularly attempt to give information about the readability level of some of their material, particularly that which is produced for 'reluctant readers'. It is wrong, however, to think of readability measurement as being important only to remedial teachers. Readability measurement is important with average and above average pupils, and teachers from all disciplines need to be able to assess the difficulty of the material which they expect their pupils to read. Reading is not something which pupils are suddenly able to do to perfection. They gradually improve their ability to assimilate more complex language and adopt different strategies. If the demands of the task are to be controlled all teachers must be able to assess the language they expect pupils of particular ability to read.

Some teachers seem to regard the attempt to assess readability as futile. They argue that they have an extensive knowledge of the child's ability, a 'feel' for language, and that they can instinctively tell what is too difficult or too easy for the child. It is true that a junior or middle school teacher who spends a large proportion of the week with a single class hears a lot of their talking and reading and sees virtually all of their writing. The teacher will doubtless form opinions as to what individuals could or could not read with ease. The secondary teacher could not hope to have such a strong foundation on which to base an assessment. However, even with junior and middle school teachers there are still problems. Even the best teachers can be wrong about what pupils can and cannot do. Sometimes they are unduly influenced by irrelevant factors such as appearance, home background and behaviour. How many clean, well-spoken children from middle-class homes have been thought to have more skill in reading than they actually possess!

Whilst it may be possible for experienced teachers to determine language that is extremely unsuitable for particular pupils, all teachers need to be able to execute a reasonably accurate match. They should be aiming at getting past the stage of saying, 'That would be far too difficult for Jason.' They need to be able to say with reasonable confidence what a pupil could read with ease. They need to be able to recognize when a book will provide just enough challenge to make demands that will stretch the pupil's present skills to the limits.

Factors in Readibility
I do not wish to spend long describing in detail the various factors which affect readability. Thorough accounts exist elsewhere – see Gilliland (1972) and Harrison (1980). However, in order to assess the weaknesses of some methods of measuring readability, and in order to appreciate the usefulness of Cloze Procedure as a method, it is useful to be aware of some of the major factors involved. I have listed these in Figure II.

Obviously some of these factors are more important than others, but what is equally obvious is that, regardless of their relative importance, the task of trying to measure them is extremely difficult.

One instinctively feels that

> When you have filled the receptacle to the brim by placing it under the tap and turning the handle in an anti-clockwise direction, terminate the water supply and cover the external surfaces of the car with water by propelling it from the bucket.

is more difficult than

> Put the bucket under the tap. Turn the tap on. Fill the bucket with water. Turn off the tap. Throw the water over the car.

but how does one quantify these feelings? It has to be said that many questions concerning readability remain unanswered. Even if factors could be quantified the answers in many cases may only be relevant and valid for particular readers. What may make a book appealing for one reader may have completely the opposite effect for another. What is needed is something which will not only gauge the factors of a book and the factors in a reader, but something which will give some sort of measurement based on the *interaction* between the reader and the book.

Figure II: Factors in Readability

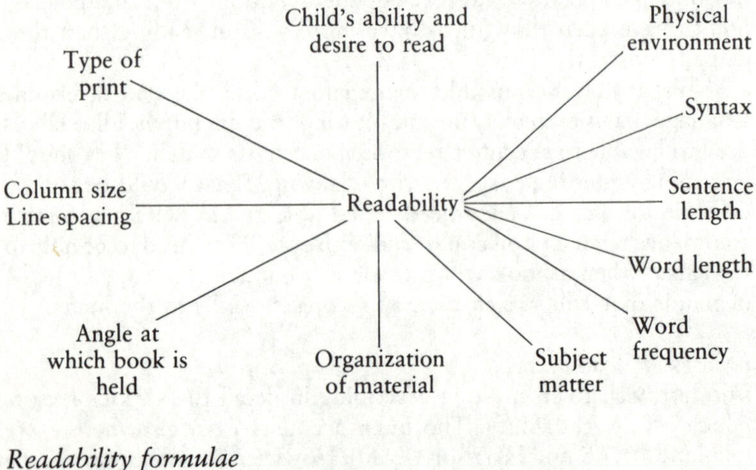

Readability formulae

Numerous formulae have been developed (mainly in the U.S.A.) which attempt to assess readability. Although some attempts have been made to incorporate personal interest factors into the formulae the three main elements used are sentence length and either word length or word frequency. Users are invited to take a sample of 100 words from near the beginning of a book and count the number of sentences in the sample. They are then instructed to count either the number of long words, (as defined by the particular formula), or the number of words which do or do not appear on a particular word frequency list. After certain numerical computations using these figures and other supplied constants, a readability level for the passage can be predicted. This procedure has to be repeated for other samples from the book, and most formulae recommend taking at least one sample from the beginning, middle and end of the book. These formulae have been developed on the basis of findings that long sentences and uncommon words contribute significantly to the difficulty which children have in reading a passage.

The Spache and Smog Readability Formulae are given below as typical examples of such formulae.

Spache
1. Select 100 words.
2. Calculate the average sentence length:
   100/Number of Sentences.
3. Count the number of words which are not on the Dale Easy Word List of 769 words. [Spache gives careful rules to guide the counting – Count all names as familiar words; count regular verb forms as familiar, irregular verb forms as unfamiliar; count adjectival or adverbial endings as unfamiliar; count plurals and possessive endings of nouns as familiar; count an unfamiliar word only once.]
4. Multiply the average sentence length by .141.
5. Multiply the number of unfamiliar words by .086.
6. Add the figures produced by 4 and 5 together and also add a constant .839.
7. The procedure is to be repeated with at least another two samples from the same book and the resulting values averaged.
8. The resulting figure corresponds to an American school grade level. This would indicate the level at which books of a similar difficulty were being read in the schools in Spache's sample.

The Spache formula was developed for use with primary material.

The following 100 words were selected at random from one of the author's short stories written for children.

> Eventually to Mrs Watson's delight, Bert leant his bike against the railings and mounted the gate. Winston was soon there, barking and nuzzling the man's legs, trying to stop his progress to the front door. Bert was forced onto the lawn and started to run. As Mrs Watson moved from the window in order to keep out of sight, and to pick up the letter, she clearly heard shouts for help. Being careful not to open the door too quickly she calmly called the dog to her side and walked up the path to meet it. It was then that (100) she realized that Winston had perhaps overdone it this time.

The Average Sentence Length $= \dfrac{100}{\text{Number of sentences}}$

$$= \dfrac{100}{5.3} = 18.868$$

Number of words outside the Dale List of 769
   Easy Words   = 19

18.868×0.141	=	2.66
19×0.086	=	1.634
Constant	=	0.839
		5.133

American grade levels can be converted into age levels by adding five. Thus it can be argued that the 100 words used above represent the difficulty of passages being read by ten-year-olds in Spache's sample.

Smog
1. Count ten consecutive sentences near the beginning of a book, ten near the middle and ten near the end.
2. In the 30 selected sentences, count every word which is three or more syllables long.
3. Estimate the square root of the number of polysyllabic words thus counted.
4. Add three to the approximate square root.
5. The resulting figure corresponds to an American school grade level. McLaughlin (1969) argued that this represents the level at which pupils from his sample scored *complete success* on comprehension tests on the passages. It represents the reading grade a person must have reached if he is to understand the text fully.

It is claimed that the Smog formula is quick and easy to apply. However, only word length is used to assess readability.

For demonstration purposes, and for ease of reference, instead of selecting 30 sentences from different parts of this book, the first 30 in this chapter were chosen.

Number of words with three or more syllables = 104

Approximate square root	=	10
Constant	=	3
		13

If five is added to the American grade level it can be seen that according to this formula, a person must have a reading age of 18 before he could fully understand the first 30 sentences of this chapter. It should be noted that McLaughlin's high criterion for reference of complete success probably makes the passage appear more difficult than it actually is.

Although readability formulae may be useful predictors of the readability level of a book it is important to be aware of some of their weaknesses when using them. First, they only attempt to quantify certain factors in readability. They ignore important aspects of text production, such as size of print. What is perhaps more significant is the fact that they ignore important factors associated with the children which influence readability, such as the children's motivational state at the time of reading and the degree of background knowledge which they bring with them to the text. Two books may have the same readability score and yet differ quite significantly in their readability because the particular readers may be more knowledgeable of, and interested in the subject matter of one rather than the other. Secondly, although they may be useful as average measures on long passages, they may yield unfortunate results on particular passages. For example, some passages may have an unusually high proportion of short words which convey difficult concepts, and this would obviously make the passage much more difficult to read than some formulae would predict. Readability formulae are general predictors of difficulty. When McLeod (1962) measured the difficulty of passages using word recognition and literal comprehension measures the results of the formulae were not always upheld. Kintsch (1974) found that the number of propositions in a sentence is a much better predictor of sentence recall than is the number of words in a sentence, and Perera (1980) argued that awareness of certain grammatical structures is more important in assessing readability than sentence length.

Even if one accepts that formulae may be inaccurate on particular passages for particular pupils, but argues that they may be generally useful, there are still problems that the user has to face. Unless the user makes the effort to discover and understand how and when a particular formula has been developed, he or she has no guarantee that the formula is reasonably accurate. Word frequency lists may be out of date, and American word frequencies will probably differ from British ones. Recently I have heard the Spache formula being recommended for use in assessing remedial material with no mention made of the fact that it was developed in 1953 using an American word list produced in 1931!

It is also important to know what criteria were selected to act as reference points for different grade levels. For example, the two formulae illustrated chose completely different criteria. Spache assigned a grade level to a sample of books according to their classroom use and worked out the correlations between these grade levels and factors in his formula. McLaughlin calculated the correlations between word length and comprehension scores on his passages, with full comprehension being the criterion for determining the particular grade. The Dale-Chall formula uses a similar technique, but the authors use a different level of comprehension success for their criterion, consequently the Smog formula usually gives a passage a higher grade of difficulty than the Dale-Chall one. It is essential to know this kind of information about the formula one wishes to use if the results are to be interpreted in a meaningful way.

A teacher who uses a formula to obtain a numerical value for a particular passage is then faced with the problem of how to use the information. What teachers need to know is how suitable a particular book is for a particular pupil or class. At best the formula result can only give them partial help. As has been noted, there are many factors which could affect the readability of the text, all of which would have been ignored by the formula. If teachers are able to make some judgement about the relative importance of these factors not included in the formula assessment, they are still left with the problem of how to use the numerical value given. It would certainly be difficult to try to correlate the value given by the formula with any 'reading age' given by a child's response on a reading test. It is well known that pupils often perform differently on different tests and that not all reading tests measure the same aspects of reading. Until both a test and formula are developed together, and standardized with a common philosophy on the same sample, it is meaningless to compare numerical values. There is no guarantee that children who are judged to have a reading age of between 9 – 9.6 years on the Schonell R1 Graded Word Reading Test will be able to read with ease a text judged to have a readability level of 9.3 years using the Spache formula. The results given by different formulae on the same passages can be alarmingly different. In a recent study Stokes (1978) applied six different readability formulae to passages taken from eleven textbooks and came to the conclusion that, even in the long run, the formulae used did not give appreciably similar results. It would seem that the match between the pupil's ability and language presented to the pupil for reading, cannot be made accurately using this method.

Cloze Readability Tests
Cloze Procedure can measure the difficulty of a text, not in terms of word length or familiarity, or of sentence length, but in terms of a particular individual's understanding of, and response to, the language structure of the text. Cloze Procedure measures a personal response to linguistic variables.

In order to be able to assess what a particular score on a cloze passage means, attempts have been made to relate these scores to certain criteria of understanding as reference points. Children's understanding of a passage, as measured by their scores on multiple-choice questions set on the passage, have been compared with the children's scores in cloze tests on the same passages. In three studies, Bormuth (1967 and 1968a) and Rankin et al (1969), involving over 300 pupils, the following criteria were adopted and used for establishing the levels of understanding that particular cloze scores represented.

1. If a child answered 90 per cent of the multiple-choice questions correctly, he was said to be able to read the passage at the *Independent Level*. He would be able to understand the language well enough to be able to cope with the language on his own.

2. If a child answered less than 75 per cent of the multiple-choice questions correctly then he would have read the passage at *Frustration Level*. The language would be too difficult for him to cope with, even if an adult were available to help him.

3. Between 75 and 89 per cent correct responses on the multiple-choice comprehension questions, the child was said to be reading at the *Instructional Level*. He would be able to cope with the language to some extent but would need assistance from an adult if he were to be able to understand the passage more fully.

By combining the figures produced in the studies mentioned above it is possible to produce approximate figures for the number of correct cloze scores that correspond to the different comprehension levels.

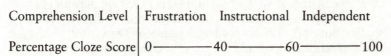

Comprehension Level	Frustration	Instructional	Independent
Percentage Cloze Score	0————40————60————100		

Before discussing the usefulness of Cloze Procedure as a readability measure in the classroom, several qualifications of the above figures need to be borne in mind. First, these figures were determined by using a particular kind of Cloze Procedure. The readability criterion scores were derived from scores on passages which had the first sentence left intact, and every fifth word thereafter deleted and replaced by a uniform size blank. Although minor mis-spellings were allowed, only the author's original word was counted as correct. Bormuth did consider the possibility of marking synonyms as being correct, but he found that, provided long enough cloze passages were used, the practice of marking synonyms correct did not significantly affect the results.

Mobley (1980), in a small-scale study, did find that synonym marking produced higher scores. Comparing exact word scoring and synonym scoring with predictions from a formula, she made the interesting suggestion that exact word scoring is more appropriate for scientific and precise subject matter, whereas synonym scoring is more appropriate for fiction. However, three points need to be made. First, the fact that cloze results produced by exact word scoring may lead to results which are surprising in the light of formulae predictions, does not necessarily mean that the cloze scores are invalid. As has been argued, formulae predictions are far from perfect. Secondly, Mobley herself points out that synonym scoring leads to subjective judgement replacing objective testing. Little is known about the reliability of individual teachers involved in synonym scoring. Thirdly, whatever the advantages and disadvantages of synonym scoring, the fact remains that in developing their criteria for judging cloze scores, Bormuth, Rankin, and Culhane used exact word scoring. If teachers wish to use their criteria it would be unscientific not to follow their recommended method.

Secondly, it is important to take a passage of sufficient length when constructing a cloze test so that the results are not unduly affected by quirks of sampling. Bormuth (1968b) suggests that passages which are at least 250 words long and which have at least 50 deletions are needed. Obviously, when assessing the readability of a book one would wish to select more than one passage for testing.

Thirdly, it must be stressed that the interpretation of cloze results using these criteria needs to be undertaken with professional skill and care. The figures of 40 per cent and 60 per cent are only an approximate attempt to conveniently combine the fruits of different research studies. Bormuth (1968a) produced figures of 44 per cent correct for the Instructional Level and 57 per cent correct for the Independent Level. Rankin et al (1969) produced figures of 41 per cent correct and 61 per cent correct respectively. One also needs to remember that the levels of comprehension to which these percentage scores have been linked have themselves been arbitarily selected. These is nothing absolute about the numbers. If one takes into account the standard error associated with any test score one can see the absolute folly of saying that because a child scored 39 per cent correct, the particular passage was too difficult for him to read, even with the help of a teacher. One may feel more confident about saying that with a score of 33 per cent. A score of 39 per cent should be used to alert the teacher to possible acute difficulty rather than be used by itself as a means for eliminating the choice of that book altogether.

Classroom Practice

Given these qualifications, Cloze Procedure is still a much more valuable tool for measuring readability than any readability formula. Because it measures the *interaction* between a child and a text, instead of simply concentrating on features in the text, it is a much more subtle measure. Taylor (1953) and Landsheere (1972) reported that cloze tests showed differences in the readability of texts which were not apparent when their readability was measured using a respected formula. The fact that caution may be required when interpreting results should not deter teachers from investing the time that Cloze Procedure requires.

There are numerous factors which will influence the choice of textbook to use with particular classes. In some cases, where a syllabus has to be rigidly adhered to, there may be little choice. There may be other compelling reasons for choosing a particular text. It could have photographs or diagrams which would be extremely useful. It may contain more recent information than its alternatives. Its presentation may be very appealing. If it is a work of fiction it may be important to read it from the point of view of literary education regardless of 'ease'. However, it may instinctively be felt by a teacher that a chosen text would present difficulty for some, if not for all of the children who would be expected to read it. The teacher needs to know answers to the following questions:

i.   Can I use it with the class provided that I do the reading?
ii. Can I expect pupils to be able to read it with understanding by themselves, for homework, for example?
iii. If it is too difficult to use with the class as a whole, who could benefit from it as a supplement to other material?
iv. If I decide to use it in class, who is going to have difficulty with it?

Suppose that you have chosen a set of books and are extremely reluctant to change them unless it is really necessary to do so. In order to answer the questions given above you randomly select three passages of at least 250 words from the book, one from the beginning, one from the middle and one from the end. When selecting your passages you also take care to start the passage at the beginning of a paragraph. The first sentence is left intact, and after that, every fifth word is deleted. You produce test sheets making sure that a uniform size gap is left where the words ought to be. If the pupils are not used to

Cloze Procedure it will be necessary to show them how to use context clues to help them guess the missing word. Once the pupils are prepared you administer the test allowing as much time as is required. Only the author's original word is marked correct, although you allow slight mis-spellings of that word.

Table I: Cloze Readability Scores

| | Results | | |
Pupil Number	Score/150	Pupil Number	Score/150
1	32	16	52
2	69	17	81
3	127	18	62
4	72	19	71
5	92	20	39
6	59	21	101
7	74	22	73
8	85	23	86
9	43	24	92
10	97	25	87
11	108	26	57
12	68	27	60
13	116	28	97
14	77	29	69
15	46	30	86

The next stage is to find out what cloze scores correspond to 40 per cent correct and 60 per cent correct. The arithmetic is fairly straight-forward, or it can be worked out diagrammatically as I have done in Figure III.

Simply by looking closely at the results in Table I and by performing a single, straightforward computation to calculate the value of the mean, much valuable information can be obtained. The mean score (see the Glossary) for the whole class is approximately 76. As can be seen from the diagram, 40 per cent correct is equal to a score of 60/150, and 60 per cent correct is equal to a score of 90/150. Therefore the average value for the class falls fairly convincingly into the *Instructional Level*. This suggests that it would be unwise to give the book to the majority of pupils in a situation where they would be expected to read it by themselves in order to gain new information. Although they may appear to be able to cope with most of the reading they would need help in reaching a more satisfactory level of under-standing. The majority of them would certainly be able to profit from

Figure III: Percentage Cloze Scores

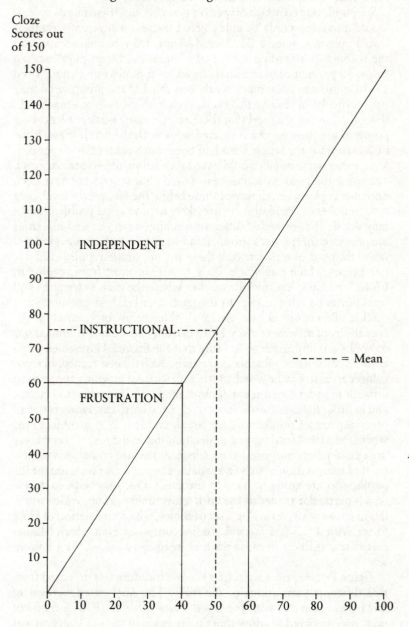

it if it were used in a classroom context, or as a means of revising something which they had already been taught.

Six pupils scored above 60 per cent correct and these pupils at least would almost certainly be able to read the text competently on their own. Pupils numbered 8, 23, 25 and 30 might also be able to cope with the reading in a reading for learning situation. Seven pupils scored below 40 per cent correct, and if one includes pupils numbered 18 and 27 there are a total of nine, nearly one third of the group, who may have difficulty in reading this book, even with the help of a teacher. In this situation one may feel that there are too many weak readers in the group to use the text in a restricted sense with the whole class. If the mean score for the whole class had been much nearer the 40 per cent level, many more pupils would have fallen below the 40 per cent level, and using the book as a class text would almost certainly have been unrealistic. However, of those falling below the 40 per cent level, only four (numbers 1, 9, 15 and 20) are likely to have acute problems. One may decide that provided different teaching strategies and materials are provided for the weak group, it may well be worth giving restricted use to the book as a class text. If there are only limited copies available one knows which pupils are likely to benefit most from reading it. Cloze Procedure has told the teacher where the class's strengths and weaknesses lie with respect to the particular book in question.

Cloze Procedure is also an invaluable means of comparing the readability of different books. If one can only afford to buy limited sets of books it is important to feel sure that the financial investments will be as educationally valuable as possible. As has been argued, in some subject areas it *may* be worth putting up with a text which appears too difficult in order to get the diagrams, maps, photographs and charts, and in order to have a more attractively produced text. However, if all other aspects of production are equal, and if it is in a subject area where the actual reading and understanding of the text is crucial, say for examination purposes, then Cloze Procedure could provide important information as to how readable the particular texts are for the pupils who are going to have to use them. One may wish to decide which particular reader to use with a low ability group, which translation to use when renewing a set of Bibles, which translation of Pliny to use with a C.S.E. Classical Studies course, or even which Mathematics text is likely to cause the least reading problems for a bottom set.

Figure IV gives the results of a Cloze Procedure test prepared from two different translations of the Bible. The *Authorized Version* of 1611 was compared with the *Good News Bible* of 1976. A friend of mine was prepared to admit that the language of the 1611 version was

Figure IV: Cloze Readability Scores for Different Bible Versions

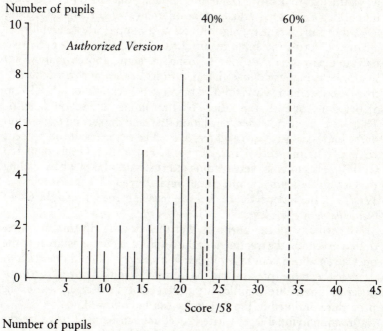

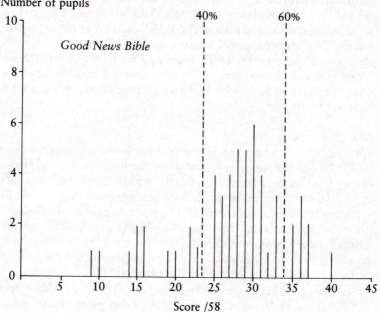

more difficult than the 1976 version, but he did not feel the difference was sufficient to justify considering changing the version in use when purchasing a new set. Because of the different styles of Biblical writing it would be an extremely lengthy process to compare the readability of all the books of the Bible in different translations. However, two narrative passages from John's Gospel, totalling approximately 300 words were duplicated in both translations and a similar procedure to that described above was followed; 55 twelve year old pupils filled in 58 deletions for each translation. No time limits were set on the tests. They were given the easier translation first, and the second translation of the same narrative a week later. According to the results 68 per cent were reading the *Authorized Version* at Frustration Level compared with 21 per cent who were reading at Frustration Level when reading the *Good News Bible*. None of the pupils coped with the *Authorized Version* at the Independent Level whereas 15 per cent read the *Good News Bible* at that level.

For virtually all the purposes that this kind of information is required in school, the treatment of the results in a manner similar to the ones given above is usually all that is necessary. Should one wish or need to be more precise and be certain that the cloze scores for different books are significantly different in a statistical sense, the procedure outlined in the Appendix can be followed.

On an individual level Cloze Procedure can be used to gauge the suitability of a single book for a single child by following exactly the same process. Admittedly the test booklet would take time to prepare, but the time invested would produce much more meaningful results than would the time invested in applying readability formulae and trying to match these results with scores obtained from reading tests. Once the passages for a book had been prepared the stencils could be kept for future use.

New Criterion Scores

Although the criterion comprehension levels have been used quite widely by reading specialists, it must be admitted that they are based on expert judgement rather than on the empirical testing of a scientific model. In his more recent work Bormuth has made suggestions for replacing the traditional criterion. The new criterion scores (Table II) are more detailed than the traditional 40 per cent and 60 per cent values (and are perhaps, therefore, less likely to be used by teachers); however, they do reflect an attempt to gauge the effect of a wide range of factors involved in the readability interaction.

Bormuth (1975) compared the cloze scores of 1600 children aged 8–17 years, with the amount of information they gained from reading the passages, their willingness to read, their perception of the difficulty of the passages, and their reading rate. The relative importance of these factors was then rated, using the judgements of 101 teachers, and the cloze scores were 'weighted' depending on whether the passages were to be used as a textbook, as a work of reference, or for voluntary reading.

Table II: Criterion Scores for Cloze Readability Tests

Use to be made of materials	Year in school									
	3	4	5	6	7	8	9	10	11	12
Textbook	59	58	57	56	55	53	52	50	50	49
Reference	55	53	52	51	49	48	47	45	45	44
Voluntary	90	62	54	50	49	46	44	40	34	34

Bormuth gave these figures as being the results of the first effort to establish rational criterion scores, and as being only approximations of the criterion scores that future research will eventually identify. Their validity and reliability can only be assessed when others have attempted to replicate Bormuth's important work. There is certainly a need for a more convincing measure of information gain to be employed in the model; also a sample of children larger than the 160 used for each age group, and the use of more than 101 teacher assessments would be desirable.

Scores which fall significantly below these criterion values suggest that the text would be unsuitable for the reader or readers. Teachers may feel more confident with these more detailed criterion scores when working with individuals. However, whether working with individuals, or with whole groups, the points made above about the professional interpretation of any cloze score need to be remembered. Standard error should make one cautious about making deceptively simple decisions based on numbers. The standard error associated with an individual's score is considerably larger than that which is associated with a class's mean score.

Before leaving the use of Cloze Procedure as a readability measure two further points need to be remembered when interpreting a cloze score. First, deletions make reading difficult and with young children or with extremely poor readers the texts may be far too difficult to yield results which can be considered meaningful. Secondly, the pooled cloze scores of a class of 30 readers will yield a much more reliable result than an individual's score. This does not mean that cloze scores are totally unreliable when considered individually. It simply means that more caution should be used when interpreting them in this way than when considering the average score for a class. As will be argued in the next chapter, there will always be a degree of error associated with any measurement.

Summary
It is important for teachers to be able to assess the readability of the language they expect pupils to read if they are to avoid causing undue frustration, or avoid failing to stretch pupils to the limits of their ability.

Readability formulae have been developed, but these only provide a crude measure of readability. They may be unreliable and need careful interpretation in the light of the date and method of their development. They cannot be used to match a child with a book.

Cloze Procedure is a much more subtle readability measure and reflects a person's understanding of a text. Cloze scores can be interpreted in the light of reference points based on different levels of comprehension. These scores enable a teacher to evaluate the readability of a book for the whole class, for the individual, and in comparison to other books.

Chapter Three

Measuring Reading Ability

Understanding Reading Tests
Whilst there are a number of hard-line sceptics who question the need
for formal reading tests, there are sadly many more teachers who place
too much faith in the wrong kind of test and who fail to appreciate the
reservations that must be made about any test result. If the usefulness
of Cloze Procedure as a means of assessing reading ability is to be fully
appreciated, then it is necessary to understand the potential weaknesses of any reading test.

Far too many teachers tend to treat results obtained from reading
tests as being an accurate measurement of some easily defined and
measurable phenomenon. These results need to be put into correct
perspective. They can only be meaningful and potentially useful to
both the teacher and pupil when questions have been asked about the
particular test's validity and reliability, and when consideration has
been given to how the result can be used.

Validity The validity of a test is the extent to which it actually
measures the entity it was designed to measure. The following are the
kind of questions that the teacher needs to ask about any reading test.

How do I know that the test actually measures what it purports to
measure? It may claim to be a reading test, but what particular
aspect(s) of reading behaviour is/are being measured? If the test is an
oral one, is the child being expected to do more than 'bark at print'? Is
he or she required to understand what is being read? If it is claimed
that comprehension is being measured could the child guess the
answers simply from reading the question, or would he or she have to
read and understand the *passage*? Do the comprehension questions
involve the reorganization of, inference from and evaluation of
material in the passage, or do they simply require literal recall? What
aspects of reading are *not* covered by this particular test? What

information is given about the test's validity? Are there any correlation coefficients given for the correlation between results obtained on this test and results obtained on other valid measures? If they are given, how high are they? How representative was the sample of children used to obtain the validity coefficients?

Reliability The reliability of a test is the extent to which it gives consistent results when applied by different people or on different occasions. Again the teacher needs to know how high the reliability coefficients are and appreciate how they were arrived at.

There are four ways of assessing reliability.

1. *Test/Retest* The same test is given to the same group of people on two separate occasions. The correlation between the sets of scores is calculated.
2. *Parallel Forms* Two equivalent forms of the same test are constructed and administered to the same group of people. The correlation between the sets of scores is calculated.
3. *Split Half* Often the test consists of only one form. It is administered to a group of people and the degree of correlation between the scores obtained on half the questions with the scores on the other half of the questions is calculated.
4. *Internal Consistency* Formulae have been developed* which take into account the different possible ways of dividing a single form test in half when calculating the correlation between pairs of scores.

The teacher needs to know how confident he or she could be that a pupil would obtain a similar score to the present one if the same test was taken not too long after the first testing.

Using the Result Assuming the test to be valid and reliable the teacher then needs to be able to answer the following questions.

What was the purpose behind my using the test? How am I going to use the information to direct my teaching to help the child's needs? Does the result show me particular areas of strength or weakness? The final decision about what test scores mean must rest with human interpretation.

Even the most complex reading tests sample only a limited range of reading skills and types of reading material. Tests can only attempt to measure how a particular person does at a particular time and place under particular conditions. It has to be acknowledged that some

---

* Such as Cronbach's Alpha Coefficient Formula and the Kuder–Richardson Formulae derived from it.

people are better at doing tests than others, and that the performance of the same candidate on the same tests may *occasionally* vary dramatically according to the time and place. In the light of all this one must regard claims that Susan has a reading age of 10 years 6 months with extreme caution. One may more accurately say that when Susan took text X on date Y under conditions Z, she obtained a score deemed to be equivalent to having a reading age of 10 years 6 months by the test author(s). Similarly if Susan scored 96 points and Peter scored 94 it would be foolish to assert that Susan was a better reader than Peter. When one remembers that there is inevitably a degree of error associated with any test score (due to the weakness of the test, the motivational state of the candidate, the conditions in which the testing took place etc.), a claim based on such a small difference would be absurd. The larger the difference, the more confident one could be that a true difference existed.

One further point needs to be borne in mind when interpreting results. A child may make significant gains in his score on a reading test after a period of instruction, but the teacher may know little about his 'progress' in the following areas which are quite crucial:

the child's attitude to reading;
the volume and quality of what is being read;
the different strategies being used when reading for different purposes.

Improved skill in 'word recognition' or 'comprehension' is only part of reading development.

Strengths of Cloze Tests

Although Cloze Tests share in some of the weaknesses associated with all reading tests, they do have several points in their favour. When wishing to assess whether or not a pupil has understood a passage it is usual to use questions to gauge understanding. Cloze Procedure avoids many of the difficulties associated with setting questions. Apart from avoiding the need to worry about setting questions which are easily understandable and unambiguous, Cloze Procedure also helps ensure that attention is fixed on a wide sample of the passage. All questions are inevitably biased in the sense that the question setter decides what is important in the passage and formulates questions accordingly. This means that some aspects of the text are 'examined' less closely than others. The deletion of words at regular intervals provokes thought and requires inference about a larger proportion of the text.

Whereas many tests examine a very limited range of reading behaviour, Cloze Procedure does require a wide range of abilities. The survey conducted for the Bullock Committee in 1973 found that 73 per cent of the primary schools sampled and 49 per cent of the secondary schools sampled used the Schonell Graded Word Reading Test. In both cases this test proved to be by far the most popular one in use. In primary schools in particular other word recognition tests were also popular. The Bullock Report concludes,

> There is no questioning the usefulness of a word recognition test for certain purposes, but so heavy a reliance on this form does suggest a narrow view of testing. (p. 251, op. cit.)

In contrast to the limited range of abilities tested by what appeared to be the most common test in use in England and Wales in 1973, it can be argued that performance on a cloze test involves the child in the following:

    i. recognising words;
    ii. using semantic, syntactic and at times stylistic information to infer and predict;
    iii. drawing meaning from outside the context of the immediate sentence;
    iv. skimming, to recap on what has been read;
    v. scanning, in search of unspecified information that may help the prediction.

So often reading tests consist of isolated words or sentences that appear slightly artificial without a context. Cloze tests supply a context for the 'questions' and require the reader to use that context to discover meaning.

Published Tests Which Use Cloze Procedure
Table III lists the standardized cloze tests which are published in this country. There are many tests available which use some form of sentence completion and two other tests are listed as examples of tests which require the reader to understand and use context in order to help them fill a gap. The purists may object that one of them, The *Schonell Silent Reading Test B*, was published before Cloze Procedure was invented. However, there are some similarities between the processes that this type of test requires and those required when completing the more usual cloze test. (Some of the similarities and differences were discussed in Chapter One.)

    There are several tests which involve children in selecting a word from a list to fit into a sentence, thus requiring them to use context to a limited extent to help them select an appropriate word. Although the *Wide-span Reading Test* uses single sentences rather than continuous

Table III: Some Tests Involving Types of Cloze Procedure

Name of Test	Author(s)	Publisher	Year	Age Range
Silent Reading Test B	F.J. Schonell	Oliver & Boyd	1944	9.0–13.0
GAP Reading Comprehension Test	J. McLeod D. Unwin	H.E.B.	1966*	8.0–12.0
GAPADOL Reading Comprehension	J. McLeod J. Anderson	H.E.B.	1973	7.3–16.11
Wide-span	M. Brimer H. Gross	Nelson	1972	7.0–15.0
Reading Level Test Part 1	N.F.E.R.	N.F.E.R. –Nelson	1970	7+ – 8+
Reading Level Test Part 2	N.F.E.R.	N.F.E.R. –Nelson	1977	9+ – 10+
London Reading Test	I.L.E.A. N.F.E.R.	N.F.E.R. –Nelson	1978	10+ – 12+

* In Australia; first UK edition 1970

prose, it does require the child to be able to choose words which are of the appropriate grammatical class as well as ones which have the appropriate meaning. Pupils are not given a list of words, all of which share the same grammatical class as the missing word. They have to use their knowledge and experience of syntax as well as meaning to select the appropriate word from another sentence. This test has two parallel forms each of which contains 80 items. The following examples are drawn from Form A.

3   No-one in the ward could draw a word out of the dwarf.

He took paper and pencil and began to ▬▬▬. 3

36   His improbable excuses made it less likely that his already doubtful listeners would believe him.

Since it seemed ▬▬▬ that the smoke would attract attention, they decided not to risk lighting a fire. 36

45   They must stand up to the   ▬▬▬ your resources when 45
     waist in water rank with   they appear plentiful, and you
     sewage and industrial waste.   may live to regret it.

77   Addressing the sceptics with   Confronted with such aston- 77
     creditable assurance he   ishing assertions, the critics
     claimed that incredible   could scarcely forbear to evince
     advances had been made   ▬▬▬ responses.
     despite the incredulous
     attitude of an obstructive
     management.

The Schonell test is now fairly old, and because of this any reading ages derived from it should be treated with extreme caution. However, it could still be used for comparative purposes. The pupil is required to select a word from a list of words which share the same grammatical class as the missing word. This could make the task less demanding than in the *Wide-span* test where the reader has to check syntactic as well as semantic correctness. However, the Schonell test does make greater demands on the memory and skimming ability as contexts of longer than a single sentence are used. The test passages each make relatively interesting reading and help to get away from the idea of the test as being a series of short, isolated sentences. The test has 42 items.

2.   They came to the church tower, and all the
        crows flew out in fright. "Caw! Caw!"
        they cried. "Go away! You must not
        peep in at our ————" (A).

     And then Tom and his friend went high, high
        up in the balloon till the church looked as
        small as a Noah's Ark and the sheep and
        the cows were like dots on the ———— (B).

     (A)   game, hat, nests, books, dinner.
     (B)   plate, river, house, trees fields.

14.   Two friends were travelling on the same road
         together when they met a bear. The one,
         in great fear, without a single thought of
         his companion, climbed up into a tree
         and hid himself. The other, seeing that

he had no chance single-handed against
the bear, had ——— (A) left but to throw
himself on the ground and feign to be dead;
for he had heard that a bear will never touch
a dead ——— (B). As he thus lay the bear
came up to his head, muzzling and sniffing
at his nose and ears; but the man held
his ——— (C) and the bear, supposing him
to be dead, walked away.

(A) nothing, something, only, perhaps, neither.
(B) fly, leap, body, horse, orange.
(C) hand, paw, coat, gun, breath.

15. When the bear was fairly out of sight, his
companion came down out of the tree
and asked what it was that the bear
whispered to him, "For," said he, "I
observed that he put his mouth very close
to your ear."

"Why," replied the other, "it was no great
secret; he only bade me beware how I
kept company with those who, when they
get into a ——— (A) leave their ——— (B)
to look after themselves."

(A) stream, difficulty, house, train, road.
(B) money, pupils, goods, friends, horses.

The *GAP*, the *GAPADOL*, the *Reading Level Tests*, and the *London
Reading Tests* employ the traditional 'open' form of Cloze Procedure,
although ever here the *GAPADOL* has some restrictions. The *GAP* and
GAPADOL were originally developed in Australia, although the *GAP*
has been restandardized in Britain. As with the Schonell test each item
is several sentences long and should therefore be more meaningful to
the pupil than a series of unrelated sentences. The reader is given a
wider context from which to make predictions. In the *GAPADOL* test
the pupil is given clues in addition to the syntactic and semantic
information by the provision of dashes to indicate the number of
letters that the deleted word has. He or she is being given an additional
criterion against which to judge his or her answer. Reprints of the
Australian version of this test have replaced the dashes with a con-
tinuous line equal in length to the number of letters that are missing,

and a similar practice may be adopted on future reprintings in Britain. Although this practice reduces the non-linguistic clues which are given to the pupil, he or she is still given some information about the length of the word required. The authors of the text have empirical evidence that the size of gap does not affect the performance of students learning English as a foreign language. However, it does not seem unreasonable to the present author to suggest that the information on word length could be used by intelligent readers who are fluent in English in helping them to choose a word for a deletion.

The *GAP* has two parallel forms containing over 30 items. The *GAPADOL* also has two parallel forms, but in this case they are much longer, each form containing over 60 items.

Two Passages from GAP Form R.

Once there was a king who had three sons. .... was called Hussein, one was called Ali and .... third son was called Ahmed. The .... also had a neice who lived .... them in the palace. She was a very beautiful .... and all three of the king's .... fell in love with her.

The first bicycles to appear on the road caused .... much sensation as the first cars. Horsemen .... for years thought of the highway as .... own special property. When cyclists came along .... challenge them, they did not like it.

Specimen Test Passage from GAPADOL Form Y.

THE IMPORTANCE OF UNDERCOATING

In applying paint of the same
colour as the original paintwork,
an undercoating − − − be omitted,
but a more durable surface will
result if two coats − − − given, as
this builds up a firm solid
foundation.

Assuming that – – – coats are to
be given, consisting of an under-
coat – – – a gloss paint, proceed
as follows:

First stir the undercoating
paint – – – – a round stick until all
the ingredients are thoroughly
– – – – – leaving no trace of sediment
in the – – – – – – of the container.
Pour out enough – – – – – to cover the
bottom of a paint "kettle", – – a
decorator's paint pot with a
handle is – – – – – –. The paint should
not be more than an – – – – deep as a
greater depth means dirty work.

The *London Reading Test* was designed to improve the provision of
information about children's reading attainment on transfer from
primary to secondary schools. The teachers and researchers who
developed this instrument have produced an extremely attractive test.
Two alternative forms are available, each measuring comprehension
by asking pupils to complete two cloze passages and answer questions
on a third unmutilated passage. There is also a practice cloze passage.
Each form of the test has 42 cloze items. The following example is the
first paragraph of one of the two cloze passages in Form A:

SNOW

The day before had been unusually frosty. The houses and cars,
coated in shining crystals of ice, had glittered and sparkled in the
sunlight as Kim made her way to ———. This morning, however, as
soon ——— she woke up, she noticed that there was something
——— about the light. The sun ——— not shining, the sky was grey,
but ——— room appeared strangely bright. Kim lay in ——— for a
moment, wondering idly ——— had changed. Then she leapt up and
——— to the window in excitement. "Snow!" ——— shouted
happily. "It must have snowed." ——— younger sister, Maria,
immediately joined her at the ———.

The test uses whole cloze passages rather than isolated sentences, thus making information available from a wide context. The marking scheme will appeal to many teachers because in several cases more than one answer is acceptable. The developers have tried to overcome the feeling that many people have that marking which counts only the author's original word as correct, is unfair. At the same time they have sought to reduce unacceptable levels of possible error inherent in synonym marking. Using the actual responses of children and collective expert judgement they have produced a list of acceptable alternative answers. Researchers who have argued that synonym marking makes little difference have been involved in using long passages in readability studies. Synonym marking on these relatively short passages in a comprehension test will give teachers more confidence in the instrument. Each passage is also accompanied by one large, cartoon-type illustration. These pictures will help to make the testing a more enjoyable and meaningful activity.

Although generally helpful in the information it gives for helping teachers interpret scores, the manuals for the test are misleading in the statements made about cloze scores and readability levels. Bormuth's later figures (Bormuth (1968a) (1968b)) have been quoted in Chapter Two of this book. Unfortunately the manual equates a score of 44 per cent correct with reading at an independent level. Because the authors have not followed Bormuth's procedure of exact word scoring they correctly point to the need for the establishment of different criteria against which scores from their test can be judged. Although they tentatively suggest alternative criteria one would wish to see more justification given before placing confidence in them.

The *Reading Level Tests* were developed to assess how well pupils can cope with prose material of known difficulty. These tests consist of eight cloze passages (four in each part) which have been graded according to Fry's Readability Chart. (Fry (1968) assesses readability using the average number of syllables and the average number of sentences in 100 words). The passages each contain between six and eight deletions. The authors have also provided a marking scheme which lists acceptable alternatives.

Information is given in the manual, which, according to the authors, would enable teachers to see if a child was reading a particular test passage at frustrational, instructional, or independent level. If the teacher then used the Fry Chart to assess the readability of other material he or she would be able to make a judgement as to the child's ability to cope with that material based on the child's performance on the test passage of similar difficulty.

Some teachers may find that the *Reading Level Tests* provide a convenient method for helping to match junior school children with appropriate material. However, considerable caution should be used when interpreting the results. No information is given about what criteria are used for establishing the particular comprehension levels. Although the manual gives a reference to Bormuth's work, presumably Bormuth's criteria are not used because the test allows synonym scoring. The authors fail to explain their criteria. It is also important to remember that the results of readability formulae and Cloze Procedure do not always agree. One may be better advised to effect matching between a pupil and a book by following the procedure for using cloze as outlined in Chapter Two than one would by using a cloze score of less than eight and a readability chart prediction. Teachers who wish to take the convenient short-cuts that these tests provide should be aware of the possible dangers.

Teacher-Made Cloze Reading Tests

In the light of the need for test users to be aware of the claimed validity and reliability of the test which they are using, it may seem strange to suggest that teachers should consider constructing their own reading tests, using Cloze Procedure. It must be acknowledged that the production of a valid and reliable reading test involves considerable professional skill, and usually also involves a lot of time, money and people. The author is not arguing that teacher-made cloze texts should, or indeed could, replace professionally developed tests on all occasions. However, there are situations where teacher-made cloze tests could be adequately used.

The average teacher is unlikely to have the technical competence necessary to develop an adequate word recognition test, but he or she would be quite capable of deleting, say, every seventh or ninth word from a passage. As has been argued, this relatively simple procedure aims to measure a much more representative sample of reading behaviour than the more complex former methods. Again, as has been pointed out, the deletion of words helps to avoid the technical problems and bias associated with question construction.

Apart from ease of construction there is evidence for the validity of cloze reading tests. Rankin (1959) reported Jenkinson as obtaining a correlation of .82 between the scores on the latter's cloze test and a multiple choice test on the same material. Jenkinson also found correlations of .78 and .73 between scores on his cloze test and scores on two standardized reading tests. Rankin (1969) reported his own work with Culhane. Correlations between their own cloze tests and multiple-choice tests on the same passages for over 100 students on five passages averaged .68. The authors point out that, in comparison to the cloze tests, the multiple choice tests took several weeks to develop. Although some of these validity coefficients are not as high as others that have been reported for some tests, they are quite encouraging when one remembers that the cloze tests were constructed simply by choosing a suitable passage and deleting words in a regular fashion. They also compare favourably with correlations obtained on a large scale between the professionally developed *GAP* Test and other professionally developed reading tests. McLeod and Unwin (1970) reported respective correlations of .67 and .72 between scores on the *GAP* Test and those on the *Schonell Silent Reading Test B* and on the *Watt's Reading Comprehension Test*.

The highest validity correlations for small-scale cloze tests have come from Bormuth (1968a, b). He constructed tests to measure the comprehension of vocabulary, explicitly stated facts, sequences of events, inferences, causal relationships, main ideas and the author's motive in each of nine passages. Scores on these tests were compared with scores of primary children on cloze tests of the same passages. Validity coefficients ranged from .73 to .84. When these correlations were corrected for the unreliabilities of the tests they approached 1.00. Using scores obtained by conventional means and cloze test scores Bormuth ranked passages in order of difficulty. He compared the rankings obtained by the two different sets of scores and obtained Spearman Rank Order Correlation Coefficients ranging from .90 to .96. It does seem that relatively unsophisticated cloze tests can be used with reasonable confidence to measure the same abilities as are measured by more conventional tests – even, it seems, in some cases where these conventional tests have been developed with considerable skill and care.

There is also evidence for the reliability of cloze tests. Using the stringent Test/Retest method for calculating reliability Taylor (1953) obtained coefficients which ranged from .80 to .88. In a large study undertaken by Landsheere (1972), twelve cloze tests of between 250 and 300 words were used with a population of nearly 4,000 French children aged between nine and eighteen. A total of 72 reliability coefficients were obtained using internal consistency methods. These coefficients ranged from .79 to .97. On a much smaller scale similar coefficients were obtained by Henry et al (1975).

Having argued that teacher-made cloze tests can be valid and reliable it must be pointed out that care needs to be taken in order to avoid obvious pitfalls. Professional judgement (perhaps aided by cloze readability information) must be used in selecting an appropriate passage. It must be a passage that the pupils to be tested would want to read, and it must be a passage that they could reasonably be expected to read. Remember that cloze deletions will add to the difficulty of the passage. If it is too difficult the test will fail to discriminate well between weaker pupils. If it is too easy it will fail to discriminate well between able pupils. Some non-fiction passages which contain a large amount of subject-specific information should be avoided. As will be argued in Chapter Seven such passages may well test the child's knowledge of that particular subject, but they may give unreliable information about the child's general reading ability. It is important to devise a test of sufficient length. As a general rule, the larger the number of items, the less chance there is of error being introduced because of poor items. Passages should be long enough to allow the deletion of *at least* 50 words. Again, *at least* the first sentence of the passage should be left without deletions. In practice, this would mean passages of at least 270 to 520 words for deletion rates from one in five to one in ten words.

It is difficult to construct a test for a group of children that have a wide range of age and ability. Teacher-made cloze tests are therefore best constructed with a fairly restricted test population in mind. A test which is specifically aimed at low-ability fifteen-year-olds, or high-ability eleven-year-olds, for example, is likely to be much more reliable than one which is aimed at every child in the school.

Once a teacher has used a home-made cloze test there is no reason why a slightly improved version could not be developed by the omission of items which are either too easy or too difficult for the population to be tested. If the test is used each year with a similar population of children, a study of the test papers will soon reveal any item which may be unsuitable and which could be removed. However, if the guidelines given above are followed it should not be necessary to remove many items, and such revisions are only likely to make slight differences to the overall validity and reliability of the test. If the test proved to be too difficult for a large proportion of the population to be tested, then a simpler passage and less stringent deletion rates could be used. If the test proved to be too easy, further paragraphs with more stringent deletion rates could be added. The teacher need not feel apprehensive about constructing cloze reading tests. With one or two revisions extremely useful instruments can be produced.

Teacher-made tests cannot be used to compare the ability of individuals or groups with national norms. The teacher-made test would have to be standardized on a large, nationally representative sample before it could be expected to provide such information. In the view of the author, teacher-made tests should not be used to make significant decisions affecting *individuals* – for example, whether a particular pupil should be moved into a particular English set. (It should be remembered that one would be extremely unwise to use the score on a professionally developed test as the sole basis for such a decision.) However, teacher-made cloze tests can be used quite legitimately in the following ways:

  i. to divide classes into smaller groups that are relatively homogenous according to reading ability;
 ii. to provide an approximate rank order of pupils according to their reading ability;
iii. to help identify the poorer readers in a class or school;
 iv. to compare the reading ability of a particular class, or group within a class, with that of other classes or groups;
  v. to help measure 'progress' in reading.

An example of a teacher-made test

The test given below, *The Day It Rained*, was constructed in order to help assess the reading ability of pupils in the top two streams in the first year of a five-form entry comprehensive school. Because of the range of ability that existed, even in the top two streams, it was necessary to construct a test which would contain items of varying difficulty. Cloze Procedure would normally produce such a range of items anyway (see Chapter Five). However, in order to increase the difficulty of certain items, the amount of available context was systematically reduced by increasing the deletion rate as the test progressed. In the first paragraph every eighth word was deleted, in the second every seventh, in the third every sixth. In the final paragraph the original plan was to delete every fifth word, but in order to make the test even more demanding and thus challenge the more able pupils, the nearest 'difficult' word to the fifth word was usually chosen.

Although many of the pupils tested had had previous experience of Cloze Procedure it was felt that a few practice items at the beginning would help increase the reliability of the test. The practice items also gave four complete sentences before the test passage started.

Instructions

  1. Say to the pupils, 'The following passage has certain words missed out. Each gap in the passage stands for just ONE word that is missing. Read the passage carefully and write in the missing word. You may find clues in the passage to help you find the missing words. If you can think of more than one word that would fit into the gap choose the one word that you think the author would have used.'

2. Help the pupils to fill in the first four gaps: answers

        for   only   from   to.

Let them give oral answers. Reject everything apart from the answers given above, explaining that rejected answers don't make sense, or that they sound wrong when read. If a pupil produces an acceptable alternative give praise, but explain that the answers given are the words used by the writer. Make sure that all the pupils have copied the first four answers into the respective gaps. Once you are happy that everyone understands what they have to do tell them to complete the rest on their own.

3. This is not a speed test and all pupils must be allowed sufficient time to complete as much of the test as they are able.

Test

The Day It Rained

It was a very rainy day. It usually rains when I'm in a hurry. I had to wait at the bus-stop ———— nearly half an hour. My mack was ———— shower-proof and it didn't stop the water ———— getting to my jumper. When it started ———— thunder I wasn't afraid, but I was ————. The trouble at school had been bad ————, but it seemed that now even the sky ———— angry with me. I couldn't help having ———— leave early in order to get to ———— opticians. It's not every day ———— your granny offers to pay for a ———— pair of glasses for you, is it!

The sky was dark ———— going almost black in places. I ———— remember looking up at the sky ———— before the first disaster happened. I ———— seen the car because of the sharp ————. I hadn't heard it coming because ———— the thunder. For what seemed like ———— a sheet of water was thrown ———— the enormous puddle at the kerb ———— my direction. I was completely drenched. ———— a sense that didn't matter as ———— was soaking wet already. But, the ———— from the kerb did finally ensure ———— the books and papers in my ———— got drenched. 'So what?' you may be thinking. 'What's the disaster in a ———— of books and papers getting wet, especially ———— they're homework books?' I agree. I ———— too put out either for a ———— seconds until I realized that apart ———— the homework books, there were also ———— written instructions on how to get ———— the opticians. My father had used ———— fountain pen that I'd bought him ———— Christmas. The ink had run everwhere ———— it completely unreadable. I was going to be late as it was. This would mean ———— I'd probably never get there at all.

———— another five minutes when the ———— eventually did arrive, I was ———— nothing else could possibly ———— wrong. I'd got into

trouble ———— school for wanting to leave ————. I'd got soaking wet
waiting ———— the rain. The history teacher ———— go mad when he
saw ———— state that 'Roman Britain" was in. ————father would be
pacing up ———— down at the opticians wondering ———— I was. I
would be wandering around looking for the ———— whose name I
couldn't remember ———— whose address I didn't know. ————
thought there was nothing ———— that could go wrong. Unfortunately
I was ————.

The bus conductor seemed friendly ———— when he asked for the
————. At least he seemed sympathetic at first. It ———— when I had
to ———— my bag out to ———— my purse that he ———— less understanding. And when ———— carefully tried to explain ————I must
have left it at ———— his pale face slowly ———— to show definite signs
of ————. While he was deciding ———— to do with me, ————
before I had a chance to ———— my wet bag, the ———— swerved
violently in order ———— avoid hitting a dog. ————, you've guessed.
The soggy ———— and papers leapt off the ———— and into the aisle.

Although teachers would not necessarily need to do this for their
own tests, some validity and reliability coefficients were calculated
to see how they compared with those given for similar tests. It is
recognized that the validity information available for this test is
limited.

Validity Scores on *The Day It Rained* were correlated with scores
obtained on the Comprehension Section of the *Richmond Tests of
Basic Skills*. The pupils had taken the *Richmond Tests* six months
before the cloze test. Table IV gives the Pearson Product Moment
Correlations between the two sets of scores.

Table IV: Validity Coefficients for *The Day it Rained*

Class	Number of Pupils	Validity Coefficient
A	30	.64
B	24	.86
Total	54	.71

What emerged from an examination of the distribution of the
scores, and the fact that the validity coefficient was lower for the top
stream than it was for the second stream, was that the test was slightly

too easy for the very able pupils. As it stands the test could be used
with all of Stream B and the majority of Stream A. However, in the
first revision of the test, additional paragraphs containing several
more difficult items are needed to help spread out the congestion of
scores at the upper end. Such a revision would be relatively easy to
execute, and the extra items would add to the overall reliability of the
test.

Reliability In addition to being used with pupils from a comprehensive
school the test was also given to a mixed-ability form of twelve-year-
olds in a private school. Internal consistency reliability coefficients
were calculated (Kuder-Richardson Formula 20.) Table V gives the
results.

Table V: Reliability Coefficients for *The Day it Rained*

School	Number of Pupils	Reliability Coefficient
Comprehensive	54	.76
Private	36	.97
Combined	90	.83

It can be seen that both validity and reliability coefficients are
reasonably high, and that they are in line with coefficients from other
similar 'home-made' tests.

The same guidelines for marking apply as those given in Chapter
Two. It is preferable to allow only the exact deleted word as being
correct. However attractive the practice of allowing synonyms may
appear at first sight, this only introduces the possibility of further test
error due to human interpretation. Provided that there is a sufficient
number of deletions the effect of scoring synonyms as correct is
unimportant. The acceptance of the exact deleted word helps to
maintain a consistent standard for the test on each occasion that it is
used.

Summary
It is important to be able to appreciate the validity and reliability of
any reading test. It is also important for teachers to have a clear idea
why they are testing in the first place. How will the results be used?
The validity coefficients are estimates of how well the test is measuring
what it claims it is measuring. The reliability coefficients are estimates

of how consistent the test is when it is used on different occasions.

All reading tests are limited in what they can do. Cloze tests do at least require a range of reading skills. Home-made cloze tests are known to be reasonably valid and reliable and teachers should consider constructing their own tests for specific groups of children to use in certain circumstances. One or two revisions of first attempts could result in extremely useful instruments.

Chapter Four

Developing Reading Ability

Introduction

So far we have considered how Cloze Procedure could help give the teacher information about a pupil's reading ability. In this chapter we will be concerned with how Cloze Procedure could be used to help children improve their reading ability. Both these themes will be taken up again in greater detail in Chapter Six.

Two points need to be stressed at the outset. First, in using Cloze Procedure as a teaching instrument, no teachers should allow themselves to think that it is a panacea for all reading problems. No such universal remedy exists. Cloze Procedure is far more than a gimmick when it is used professionally, but at the same time it is only one activity among many that teachers may want to introduce as part of a reading development programme.

Secondly, it has to be remembered that although there seem to be many sound arguments as to why Cloze Procedure ought to improve aspects of reading performance, there have been criticisms of using it as a teaching instrument. In summarizing the work done up to 1970, Jongsma (1971) showed that most of the studies had failed to show any improvement in reading due to Cloze Procedure. This may have been for at least three reasons. First, some of the studies exposed children to Cloze Procedure for comparatively short experimental periods. For example, in a study by Louthan (1965) pupils were given only six exercises to complete. Secondly, many of the studies gave the pupils no training in how to use context clues. Thirdly, most of the studies up to 1967 simply asked subjects to fill in cloze passages without involving any group discussion or feedback from the teacher. However, there have been studies which indicate the usefulness of Cloze Procedure. Harrison (1980), in his review of the literature, quotes a study by Martin done in 1968, in which a nine-week programme of cloze exercises produced significant gains in reading ability. In this study the subjects had been asked to explain their choice of word. Studies by Kennedy et al (1973) and by Samuels et al (1974) indicate that certain applications of Cloze Procedure can help remedial readers. Henry et al (1975) claimed an improvement in the reading ability of a sample of French children due to Cloze Procedure. It should be noted that in this latter study there was a large discussion element between the teacher and pupils in the experiment. Jongsma has recently published a review of American instructional cloze studies which have been conducted since his first report (Jongsma (1980)). In contrast to the nine studies reviewed to 1971, his latest work encompasses 36 empirical studies, of which 26 were conducted as part of doctoral theses. Concerning the studies specifically related to reading comprehension Jongsma concluded that cloze was equally as effective as traditional methods. He also found that cloze instruction which is carefully sequenced in length and difficulty, and adjusted to the reading abilities of the students, is more effective than the undifferentiated use of cloze exercises. This latter point will be developed in the next chapter. In addition to the experimental evidence, published recordings of groups of pupils discussing cloze passages, (Lunzer and Gardner (1979), Rye (1980)) illustrate the clear potential for developing certain reading skills that this practice has.

Cloze and Intermediate Skills

If we imagine the reading process to involve a whole range of skills, at one level there would be the ability to decode graphic signals given by letters, and on a higher level there would be the ability to understand, organize and reason with meaning. Somewhere between these two levels would be what Merritt (1969) has called the Intermediate Skills, and by this term he means the ability which enables a reader to read *fluently*.

> A mere mastery of the primary skills does not, of course, represent the ability to read. Comprehending, evaluating and organizing new facts, impressions and ideas – these are the very essence of reading. . . . But what of fluency? Where does this fit into the picture? After all, there are many children who can achieve high scores on word recognition tests, and who can even comprehend what they so painfully read, but who read haltingly, often one word at a time. . . . On the one hand . . . it would appear that . . . the ability to recognise words is no guarantee of fluency. On the other hand it is clear that the skills which underpin fluency are relatively independent of higher order skills.

Children's fluency in reading depends on their ability to make use of certain clues in the context to help them predict what words are going to come next. In this way the reading process is not slowed down by the child having to spend a long time in focusing on every word.

Fortunately letters and words do not occur in random order. They frequently occur together in particular combinations. Familiarity with these combinations helps the child to predict which letter or word may be coming next in a particular sequence. Once part of a sequence is given it is relatively easy for a fluent reader to complete it. In the following sequence once the first two or three letters have been given, most readers could guess the word.

n   ni   nig   nigh   night

Apart from frequency of occurrence in collocation with other words, there are also important constraints acting on words. Meaning and grammatical rules powerfully determine which particular words might follow in any given sequence.

He got into the car and turned on the ———

Understanding of the situation and previous experience of language would enable most readers to predict 'ignition' as the missing word. Whatever word was suggested, grammatical considerations would rule out anything that was not a noun. As the child becomes more skilful in making hypotheses about what is to come next on the basis of what has gone before, his or her fluency will increase accordingly.

It has been argued by Merritt (1969) and by Walker (1974) that Cloze Procedure is one way of helping a child develop an awareness of sequence and of the semantic and syntactic clues which help prediction, as well as giving practice in making predictions.

Cloze, Scanning and Search Reading

The skilled reader does not read all printed matter in the same way. A bus timetable is usually read in a different way from the way in which a person would read a novel. Users of a timetable are looking for particular information. Their eyes are made to pass quickly over a large amount of information that is quickly rejected because they know it is not what is wanted. When the reader's eyes receive the appropriate visual clues they stop scanning and the person reads the relevant information carefully. On the other hand, when reading a novel the reader may read at a fairly uniform pace for some sections, interspersing these periods with pauses for careful reflection about the text, and possibly periods of very quick reading to find out what happens next. The range of reading skills that mature readers employ can be further illustrated by showing what happens when they look something up in a reference book. Such readers would first scan the index for page information. Having located the page, they would skim the page quickly until the relevant passage was located. Then they would read this passage and even re-read it with great care. They might engage in some form of 'dialogue' with the text by asking questions which arise from the reading, or reorganize the material in the form of notes or a summary.

Pugh (1978) defined the particular skills of scanning and search reading as follows:

> Scanning is used within a text to locate a specific symbol or group of symbols (such as a particular phrase, formula, name or date.) The reader knows what the symbol or group of symbols looks like, and therefore, he also knows when he has located what he is seeking. In his visual activity the reader exhibits a mixture of rapid inspection of the text with an occasional closer inspection. He may not read line by line and may well, in a book, disregard the author's sequencing. . . .
> Search reading is a more demanding mental activity since here the reader is attempting to locate information on a topic when he is not certain of the precise form in which the information may appear.

Traditionally attention in schools has been given to developing understanding of the text, and other skills have been neglected. Cloze Procedure could be one way of developing scanning and search reading abilities. Although the authors of the manual for the Edinburgh Reading Test, Stage 4 (1977) may differ slightly from Pugh in their terminology, they suggest that Cloze Procedure could be used to remedy low scores achieved by pupils in the section of their test which tests the skill described by Pugh above. When faced with a blank space to fill in pupils are not simply faced with blank paper, but with blank paper that is surrounded by syntactic and semantic clues to help them guess. Pupils who are trained to look for information instead of guessing in an apparent vacuum will inevitably be employing the reading skills outlined above. They will be searching, not necessarily following the order of the author's sequence, looking for clues that their memory tells them are present, and looking for material that may provide a basis for a guess. If they attempted to look for information by re-reading the whole passage at the normal rate each time, following the precise order of the text, the process would become extremely tedious and would soon be abandoned.

Cloze, Comprehension and Group Discussion

The purpose of setting comprehension questions on any text, whether it be in an English lesson or in any other subject area, is to direct the reader back into the text, to help the pupil think through some of the implications of what has been written and to help them understand the full meaning of what has been printed. Whatever one believes about whether or not comprehension is a multiplicity of aptitudes, it seems essential that teachers should get beyond asking questions which demand a simple literal understanding of what the writer has written. Situations need to be created where pupils are asked to make inferences about the implicit meanings of individual words and about the implications and value of whole arguments and passages. We need to develop perceptive, reflective readers.

Cloze Procedure is one way in which the ability to infer implicit meaning could be developed. Look carefully at the following extract which was transcribed from a recording of four pupils discussing a cloze passage. The four girls were all in the top stream of a first year in a comprehensive school. They had already discussed the italicized adjective.

> But on that cold, *darkening* evening the twilight had fallen early. It was almost dark by now and even the landscape near him was . . . The wind had grown stronger while he rode and it gave the countryside a strange life of its own. (*Reading Beyond The Lines*, E. Williams, Arnold.)

Natasha: It was almost dark by now and even the landscape near him was strange.

Cherry: Foggy.

Helen: No.

Cherry: It was foggy.

Helen: No . . . uh . . .

Cherry: It was foggy.

Helen: It was half . . .

Natasha: He can't see it very well.

Helen: Unclear.

Cherry: Misted . . . misted. Yeah, misted.

Natasha: Sort of when you look . . . sort of . . . sort of looks like a mist.

Sarah: Yeah.

Natasha: Twilight looks like mist.

Helen: Yeah, because of the landscape.

Cherry: It was foggy.

Helen: It was almost dark by now.

Sarah: The wind had grown stronger while he rode and it gave the countryside a strange life of its own.

Helen: Unclear.

Natasha: No . . . Unclear . . . You can't just say unclear. Unclear could be anything . . . could be raining or anything. It sort of . . . looks . . . when he looks at it he couldn't make out the shapes of anything.

Cherry: Unnoticeable.

Sarah: Unnoticeable wouldn't go.

Helen: It would.

Natasha: Yeah, but look, you couldn't say . . . It was almost dark by now and even the landscape near him was unnoticeable. It wouldn't sound right 'cos it would mean that he couldn't see any.

Helen: He would notice it.

Natasha: He would notice it, but it would be sort of blurred.

Cherry: Misty.

Sarah: The landscape near him was blurred.

Cherry: Blurred.

Helen: Blurred!

Natasha: Yeah, 'cos look, if you look down you can see the sort of shapes, but you can't see the actual things.

Sarah: Blurred.

Natasha: Blurred.

Cherry: How do you spell blurred?

As it happens, in this particular case, the word chosen by the group is the same as the word in the original. However, in the light of the discussion produced by the group it can be seen that the 'correct' answer is only of secondary importance. Nevertheless, the fact that the group did produce a relatively unusual word like 'blurred' in this context demonstrates that they were able to appreciate the subtle meanings of the context.

The group was faced with two problems, namely the discovery of the general semantic field from which the missing word would come, and the choice of a particular word to suit the context in question.

They seem to have solved the first problem relatively easily. They managed to infer from the given context that they were looking for a word to describe the rather hazy conditions which existed on the rocks. It is an appreciation of these conditions which contributes to the ghostly atmosphere that the author is attempting to create in the context which follows the given passage. This inference is not coherently stated in this particular example, but the suggestions which the girls offer all indicate that they have a clear idea of the man's situation.

Some of the suggestions are never explicitly rejected. This may be due to social tact and the fact that new ones are quickly suggested and taken up before time has been allowed for the rejection of the old ones. Other alternatives *are* explicitly rejected on the grounds that they are semantically imprecise and inappropriate for this context.

Although one girl in particular does a lot of talking it would be wrong to assume that she does all the work. Natasha is used as a sounding board for suggestions made by other members. As she gives reasons for rejecting 'unnoticeable' she suggests a better word, but in a different context. This word is immediately taken up by Sarah who 'sounds out' the word in the passage context. Natasha then supports Sarah with a reasoned defence.

A cloze passage has been used by the group as a basis for a discussion about word meanings. All through the discussion a thoughtful awareness of the context has underpinned that discussion. In the following example context is used even more overtly as a means of justification. Three sixteen-year-old boys of average reading ability were discussing an extract from *Kipps* by H.G. Wells. Again, as it happens, they succeed in choosing the word given by the author.

> On Sunday he was obliged to go to Church once, and commonly he went twice, for there was nothing else to do. He sat in the free seats at the ———; he was too shy to sing . . .

Derek:	He sat . . . in the free seats . . . at the church.
Robert:	He sat in . . .
Peter:	No, that'd be . . . that wouldn't be the church would it? That would be . . .
Robert:	Tabernacle.
Derek:	At the church. At the church. Where else would he be? He was going to the church wasn't he. At the church. He was too shy to sing . . .
Robert:	He sat at the back.
Derek:	and not always good enough . . .
Robert:	No.
Derek:	to keep his word . . . word . . .
Robert:	Hey! . . . What I . . . He sat in the free seats at the back. Could be.
Derek:	In the free seats . . .
Peter:	In the free seats at the . . . I don't think there would be . . .
Derek:	At the church.
Peter:	At the church because you know he go to the church already don't you.
Derek:	It could be at the back, front . . . anywhere.
Peter:	Middle.
Derek:	Middle.
Robert:	He sat in the free seats . . .
Derek:	Sat on the ceiling . . . could be anywhere. It's got to be church. It's the only place you know where he is.
Peter:	He'd go to the back though. He only goes 'cos he's nothing else to do.
Derek:	He's shy, so he'd just sit at the back.

Peter: He'd sit at the back.
Derek: Yeah . . . could be back . . . because . . . Ah yes! Because
            he was too shy to sing.
Peter: Yes, at the back.
Derek: Yes . . . too shy to sing.

'Church' would fulfil the semantic requirements of the sentence in a general sense, and this comes close to being accepted. Finally, however, information in the context is used as a basis for inferences about how this character would act in the situation in question. This narrows the semantic field and a more appropriate word is chosen. Cloze Procedure has made these pupils read carefully and reason together about meaning.

Training
In their study of groups of children discussing together in order to learn, Barnes and Todd (1977) found that their groups spend time re-interpreting the set questions in their own terms and in clarifying what the teachers wanted them to do. Because in one sense Cloze Procedure presents a less open-ended task, pupils who have received training in how to do a group cloze task spend very little time in deciding how to go about the task. Most of their energy is directed into the demands of the passage.

The question of training is also important in other respects if maximum benefit is to be derived by the pupils when using Cloze Procedure in this way. Anyone who listens to a group of pupils discussing a cloze passage may find that the quality of the discussion is not always so obviously valuable as it is in the examples given above. This finding may be attributed to *at least* four factors, namely, the passage itself, the type of deletions made, inability to use context clues and inexperience in group discussion. The first two of these factors will be discussed at length in the next chapter. The importance of the latter two in limiting the effectiveness of Cloze Procedure unless training is given can be seen by looking closely at how pupils 'naturally' use context in a cloze situation.

An analysis of a transcript of 600 utterances given during a group discussion of a cloze passage suggested that answers are sought at both a conscious and subconscious level using context. Some context usage consisted of a pupil simply saying a word or two immediately next to the deletion. The words in the immediate context are usually repeated by other members of the group until finally the missing word which completes the linguistic segment is found. Production of the missing word is often attempted at a subconscious level first. The pupil hopes that previous experience of similar language structures will produce the missing word. At this stage he or she is not consciously searching the context or consciously going through rules of grammar to arrive at a logical guess. Rational strategies are only tried when the intuitive one fails.

When compared to the deliberate use of more distant context, this particular usage of immediate context may appear disappointing, but it should not surprise us. Language is perceived in relatively short linguistic segments (Fodor et al 1965). When a word is missing it is only natural that the immediate context should provide the first source of help. Other studies (MacGinitie (1961) and Alderson (1979)) have shown that the ability to fill in a cloze deletion correctly does not improve significantly as the amount of immediate context increases, once a context of five words is given. It would seem that the strongest constraint on words is supplied by the immediate context. It should be remembered that Cloze Procedure in these latter studies involved individuals filling in cloze passages in silence. Although the results show where the strongest constraint lies they do not necessarily prove that pupils cannot be trained to use a wider context.

The fact that groups often repeatedly read the context aloud to themselves is also consistent with what we would expect from research findings. Hardyck et al (1970) found a relationship between laryngeal activity and the comprehension level of the passage. Their findings support the interpretation that as the pupil finds the cloze passage difficult to read he or she produces additional stimuli to help understanding and the production of the missing word. The auditory stimuli of the voice are reactivated by the pupil to help him or her cope with the difficult material.

It should be clear that training is essential if the pupils are to get beyond this first stage of only sounding the immediate context. They need to be shown how to look for syntactic clues, and in particular, how to look for semantic clues beyond the immediate context. The teacher also needs to encourage pupils to provide a reason for the choice of their word. It may be that the justification has to be searched for *after* a suitable word has been subconsciously generated from the immediate context. Pupils will find this strange and difficult at first but they will become more skilful with practice.

Groups
No rigid rules can be given about the size and make-up of the discussion groups. The teacher needs to be flexible in the light of his or her knowledge of the particular children concerned. Walker (1974) has argued that with a group of less than eight children there would be

little opportunity for a range of views to be expressed, and that a group of twelve and over is far too large for all individuals to have the opportunity to contribute. In my own experience with secondary children I have found that groups of three or four children work best. Barnes and Todd (1977) also suggest that groups of two, three or four are the optimum size for discussion groups for children in the eleven to fifteen age range. In their research they found that discussion groups of more than four usually resulted in one or more members remaining silent. They also argued that where the time available for discussion is limited, as in a classroom situation, the addition of several members to a small group of four means less time available for each member to talk. They go on to write:

> . . . we also believe that to have a fifth or sixth member imposes strains on the social organization of the group which diverts the children from the main task. The basic task of ordering the discourse – who talks, and when – becomes too difficult for children who are used to being controlled by the teacher.

Because we naturally talk most to those with whom we are best acquainted it is important to let pupils select their own small groups to start off with. This practice will almost certainly result in groups which are fairly homogeneous with respect to the sex and ability of their members. However, as pupils become accustomed to working in groups and accustomed to the cloze task, the teacher may wish to deliberately select groups which are mixed according to sex, and which reflect a wider range of ability than may have been reflected in the peer groups.

Marking

When using Cloze Procedure as a means of developing reading skills it is *not* necessary for the teacher to insist on an exact match between the author's word and the word offered by the pupils before credit is given. The value of the exercise lies in the thought and discussion that goes into arriving at an answer rather than in the 'correct' answer itself. Having said this, one would obviously need to point out any answers that were syntactically or semantically unacceptable, particularly in subject areas other than English where there may be a definitely 'right' answer. However, there are usually several deletions which allow more than one possible answer and in discussing the different answers provided by the groups, the marking can become a teaching exercise. In the sentence

The old man and his dog ———— walking down the road.

the missing word is clearly 'are' or 'were'. Groups which allow 'is' or 'was' to go uncorrected need their attention drawn to certain grammatical conventions. However, in the sentence

The old man and his ——— were walking down the road.

a pupil who puts 'wife' instead of 'dog' may deserve credit if there is nothing in the context to definitely indicate that the word must be 'dog'. If there is, the teacher can point this out and thus provide a reason for his rejection. In effect the teacher is joining the group and using his or her superior perception to point to weaknesses in the group's reasoning. Where acceptable alternatives are provided by the group the teacher may wish to discuss the possible reasons for the author's choice of his particular word. With sensitive 'marking' the teacher can ensure that the learning process continues *after* the passage has been completed.

Summary

There are three areas in which it has been claimed that Cloze Procedure can help develop general reading ability, namely in the intermediate skills, in scanning and in comprehension.

Pupils are able to infer quite subtle meanings from cloze passages in discussion together. It is argued in this chapter that the success of group cloze discussion activities depend, in part, on the instructions given to the pupils and their experience of group discussion. Pupils must understand the need to give a reason for their choice of word to fill the deletion. This helps them to think about the context beyond the immediate linguistic segment. It is recommended that small groups be used for discussion.

The teacher can help the learning process continue after the group discussion by giving credit for appropriate, as well as correct responses, and by explaining possible reasons behind the author's choice of words.

Chapter Five

Some Factors in Passage Preparation

Introduction

It has been claimed that cloze passages are easy to prepare. After all, what could be simpler than deleting a few words? When seeking to develop comprehension, all the inferential questions (which are difficult to set) can supposedly be left unformulated and be replaced with uniform-sized blanks. Perhaps it is this apparent ease of preparation rather than effectiveness or versatility which has made Cloze Procedure appealing to some teachers.

In some areas cloze passages are certainly much easier to prepare and execute than their alternatives. When measuring readability the deletion of every fifth word only requires the ability to count and does not require the more lengthy computations involved when using some readability formulae (although it must be admitted that the physical reproduction of the passages will take time). In the area of testing previous knowledge of a subject (see Chapter Seven), it is far easier to delete some content words than it is to set successful questions on the passage. However, when it comes to using Cloze Procedure as a means of encouraging readers to think about the passage, the passage itself, and the way in which it is prepared, are crucial to the success of the task. Although the job of preparing passages for Cloze Procedure is not a particularly difficult one, if the passage is to be effective, more is involved in its preparation than simply choosing a portion of language in a busy 'free' period and deleting every nth word. As in all effective learning situations, professional skill and care are involved. However convenient the concept of deleting every nth word is, it is too inflexible. Children's interaction with language is far too complex and sensitive for them to be given passages which have not been skilfully prepared. It must be remembered that we are trying to encourage children to read in order to *learn*.

In the previous chapter I tried to show how various factors in the cloze task could affect performance. I now wish to discuss the effect that the removal of particular words has on the task and consequently show how the teacher can gradually increase the demands being made on the reader.

A Suitable 'Raw' Passage

Teachers are continually trying to make a happy match between the reading ability of their pupils on the one hand, and the difficulty and appeal of the language that they present to pupils on the other. This matching is no less important when it comes to considering passages to be used in Cloze Procedure. In fact, there are at least two reasons why the matching is even *more important* when selecting passages for deletions.

First, by deleting words, the teacher is making the reading task more difficult than it ordinarily would be. It is therefore important to encourage the motivation of pupils with an interesting passage. It is almost as if the interest value of the passage has to compensate for the disruption in eye movement and greater burden on the memory that the deletions will cause. Some have suggested that the cloze task in itself generates interest and encourages motivation. This may be true for some pupils who are new to cloze, or for able and articulate children who enjoy being challenged, but it would be foolish to assume that the task automatically has an attraction for the majority of pupils. The passage should be one which the pupils both could and would want to read. A passage which is too difficult and which does not appeal in the first place is not likely to be enhanced by having words removed.

Secondly, the cloze task depends very heavily on the passage itself to motivate the pupil into filling in the gaps in a meaningful way. In ordinary reading exercises there are questions at either the beginning, or more usually the end of the passage which can act as a stimulus to thought and as a means of encouraging the reader to read, and even re-read with a purpose. Questions are familiar. They are the kind of task that pupils are used to doing and pupils usually understand what is expected. If questions are not answered satisfactorily, or even attempted, then it is easy for the teacher to see that very little has been achieved and to act accordingly. However, when using Cloze Procedure to generate thinking about a passage the stimulation of a deletion is not necessarily so helpful or specific as that of a question, and it is not so easy to detect 'fraud'. It is possible for pupils to fill in blanks in a reasonably accurate way and yet achieve very little. If the pupils start playing the game of 'fill-the-blanks-to-keep-teacher-happy-and-keep-us-out-of-trouble' it is far less obvious that little thought had gone into the process than would be the case if short and shallow written answers were produced. Although other factors are involved, the standard and interest value of the passage are extremely important in motivation, and thus in determining the amount of thinking, careful reading and discussion that goes on when filling deletions. Again, it needs to be stressed that when using Cloze Procedure in this way, what goes on in reaching the answer is as important as the answer itself.

The precise nature of the difficulty caused by different deletions will be the main concern of the rest of this chapter. As a general point it is worth noting at this stage that the language of the passage should not be beyond the independent reading level of the children before deletions are made from it. If the unmutilated language would cause any difficulty, then the further difficulty that would be caused by deletions would result in the pupils becoming frustrated and alienated from the task. Experience of using Cloze Procedure as a readability measure, as described in Chapter Two, will help develop skill in assessing the difficulty of the passage.

Word Class

Look carefully at the following sentences and notice how the grammatical class of the word which has been deleted affects the relative difficulty of the task.

1　A man and ——— woman stood on the bridge.
2　People ——— queueing to go into the cinema.
3　Robert picked up the gun. ——— aimed it at the window.
4　Most people enjoyed the book, ——— some didn't.
5　A man and a woman ——— on the bridge.
6　People were queueing to go into the ———.
7　Robert picked up the gun. He aimed it at the ——— window.
8　Most people ——— said that they enjoyed the book.

You probably had very little difficulty in supplying 'a', 'were', 'He' and 'but' for sentences 1, 2, 3 and 4 respectively. You may have preferred 'the' for 1, 'are' for 2 and 'though' for 4, but apart from minor variations it would be relatively easy to obtain answers for the first 4 sentences that the vast majority of people would agree with. However, the same could not be said for sentences 5, 6, 7 and 8. In the light of the preceding context you may wish to put 'stood' in 5. But why not 'were', 'sat', 'sang' or 'laughed'? Why not 'shop' instead of 'cinema' for 6? The possibilities for 7 and 8 are equally plentiful. Even when more context is supplied it may still be impossible to arrive at a satisfactory answer with any degree of certainty that the word chosen is the same as the one deleted.

Language involves highly complex behaviour, allowing very many possible sentences, yet at the same time having rules governing the structure of all sentences. These rules generate structure words which are common to many sentences. This means that in any given sequence of words some are bound to be more predictable than others. Although the distinction between words which mainly determine structure and carry grammatical information, (e.g. articles, prepositions, conjunctions and auxiliary verbs) and words which convey the main bulk of meaning (e.g. nouns, verbs, adjectives and adverbs) is a crude one, it is a useful distinction for our purposes.

The measurement of the relative difficulty of prediction of each word class has been carried out quite simply, by giving large numbers of undergraduates cloze passages with every nth word deleted. Answers were then analysed according to word class and correctness. Aborn et al (1959) and Fillenbaum et al (1963) found that there was an order of difficulty according to word class when it came to finding the correct answer:

Figure V: The Difficulty of Prediction of Different Word Classes

	articles, auxiliary verbs, prepositions, conjunctions	STRUCTURE WORDS
DIFFICULTY		
	nouns, main verbs adverbs, adjectives	CONTENT WORDS

When one considers the number of words covered by the class 'noun' and compare that with the number of words in any of the structure word classes, it is not difficult to see part of the reason for the relative ease of prediction of structure words. There are simply fewer of them to choose from and therefore the chance of success is statistically much higher. However, the relative size of grammatical class is not the only factor affecting the predictability of that class. Class frequency is also important. An analysis of class frequency of words in sentences taken from American popular magazines (Aborn et al (1956)) showed that as a broad class, structure words occurred more frequently than any other class:

Figure VI: The Frequency of Different Word Classes

↑ Structure words

Nouns and pronouns

FREQUENCY Main verbs

Adjectives

Adverbs

Note the approximate inverse relationship that exists between difficulty of prediction and frequency of occurrence (see Figures V and VI.) It appears that greater familiarity with a possible correct answer makes the task of selecting an answer much easier.

Apart from the relative predictive difficulty of each class per se, the teacher must also keep an overall perspective when deciding which deletions to make. Word class not only affects the difficulty of each deletion but each class contributes differently to a *cumulative* effect. The control of this longer-term effect is also crucial if the passage is to assist in pupils' learning. If mainly important content words are deleted it is obvious what the effect will be on the sentence and on the passage as a whole.

1 The tall ——— quickly ——— the ———.
2 ——— ——— man ——— robbed ——— bank.
3 ——— ——— giraffes ——— ate ——— leaves.

Even though sentences 2 and 3 have a higher deletion rate than sentence 1, and even though sentence 1 does contain some content words, 2 and 3 make more sense than 1 does. Nouns and verbs are particularly important in conveying meaning. Thus, although adverbs are particularly difficult to predict, a passage with mainly nouns and verbs deleted would be far more difficult to make sense of than one which had mainly adverbs missing. The class which is easier for a particular deletion may make the overall task too demanding for the pupil. Admittedly, something of the content is lost by the removal of adjectives and adverbs, but at least the actors, actions, processes and states remain.

Finally, it is important to remember that nouns and verbs do contain obvious grammatical information as well as meaning. The number of a noun obviously influences the verb and vice-versa. Verbs also contain information about tense. The teacher must be careful not to remove words which are grammatically mutually dependent unless clues remain as to what either of the dependent words is. The removal of both the italicized words from the following sentence would mean that if the sentence were taken in isolation, either one of them would be impossible to guess without the other:

The *women* from the home *are* going out.

By supplying the 'women' one is exerting important constraint on the auxiliary verb. We know that it must be plural. However, we still do not know the tense. If 'are' were supplied instead of 'women' we would be given both tense and number information. Whatever the merits of deleting either, both should not be chosen for deletion together.

It should be apparent by now that word class is a major variable that the teacher can control and use to gauge the difficulty of the task to suit his or her particular group. Before illustrating the practical implications of these ideas it is necessary to mention two other variables. Although deletion position and length of context do not *always* exert such obvious constraint as word class, they do exert influence and *can* be very important.

Word Position

1. The conductor, the string players, the brass players and the percussionists all rushed to the concert hall in order to give a ———.

2. The ———, the string players, the brass players and the percussionists all rushed to the concert hall in order to give a performance.

Although it is difficult to be sure, the last word of the first sentence is probably more predictable than the earlier word of the second. This cannot be attributed to word class alone as both the deletions are nouns.

Language is sequential. In the normal course of reading, the beginning of a sentence sets up expectations about what is to follow. The reader forms certain hypotheses on the basis of the information received from the beginning of the sentence, and these are either confirmed or rejected, depending on the further information that the mind receives. By looking at the sentence given above it is easy to see how the constraint that is exerted on what is coming next seems to increase steadily towards the end of the sentence. Once the words in the first half of the sentence have been read correctly the remainder of the sentence follows quite easily.

Words which occur at the beginning of a sentence are usually more difficult to predict if they are removed, than words of their equivalent class later on in the sentence. (The possible exception to this is in passive sentences.) Again, nouns in particular are important. Studies involving short-term memory have shown that if subjects are briefly shown a sentence and asked to reproduce it later, it is the nouns at the beginning of the sentence which are reproduced most accurately. The nouns are most influential in determining the thematic possibilities of what is to follow. Obviously the theme could be inferred from the end of the sentence, but this is the reversal of the normal process. In such an easy sentence as

The ———— marked the exercise books.

It is possible to infer 'teacher', but only by working backwards after reading the whole sentence. This is more difficult than predicting 'books' in

The teacher marked the exercise ————.

It must also be remembered that at the beginning of a sentence there is not always a previous helpful context to help anticipation. This may be because the sentence concerned is at the beginning of a pargraph or of a passage. It is more likely to be because the previous sentence does not always provide strong, specific constraint on the opening noun of the following sentence.

Both prosecutor and defendant had their reasons to be dissatisfied. The ———— was . . .

We cannot be sure about the constraint that the first sentence may have on the opening noun of the second. It could be either 'prosecutor' or 'defendant'. Some may wish to argue that it ought to be the former because it comes first in the previous sentence. On the other hand it might be something completely different – 'judge' for instance. After reading ahead the reader would be able to get valuable clues to help him or her decide, but very little is gained from the previous sentence. Usually constraint within a sentence is much stronger than constraint between sentences. In sentences words are constrained both by meaning and by grammar. The only constraint between sentences is one of meaning, concerning the possible meaning of the next sentence.

As would be expected, words deleted from the ends of sentences are more predictable than words of their equivalent class deleted from the beginning. The reader's hypotheses are continually confirmed or modified as he or she progresses along the sentence. Consequently the semantic and syntactic foundations behind the prediction of a word at the end of a sentence are much stronger than for one at the beginning. The strength of the constraint increases with sentence length up to a point.

Studies already referred to, which have used Cloze Procedure as a tool for measuring the predictability of word classes and their distribution in sentences have found that the last word in a sentence is not necessarily the most predictable. This is because the last word is rarely a structure one. Thus although the constraint on the final content words exceed that on the content word at the beginning, the greater constraint appears to be on the structure word prior to the final content word.

Using 24 highly verbal undergraduates and over 1000 sentences, Aborn et al found that words deleted from the middle of the sentences were more predictable than words deleted from either the beginning or the end. It appears that a context either side of a deletion is more constraining than a context of one side only.

Figure VII: Position in Sentence and Difficulty of Prediction

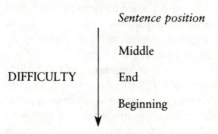

One possible explanation for this is that the first half of the sentence is long enough to provide a strong foundation for an accurate guess. The second half of the sentence may act as a powerful check on the hypothesis. This check would be far more effective and constraining than one that might be provided by a consecutive sentence on a word deleted from the end of a former sentence. It may also have something to do with the fact that there is a greater chance of a structure word occurring in the middle than in either end position in the sentence.

Length of Context
Before deciding on which words to delete one further factor needs to be understood. Constraint is affected by the length of context. Various attempts have been made to measure the relationship between length of context and constraint. Obviously any measure of the amount of context which gives maximum constraint, whether it is given in words or letters, is bound to be a relatively crude approximation. This must vary from situation to situation. A mere number cannot take into account the subtle and varied constraint exerted by both meaning and structure that will be different for each sentence.

Although the importance of bilateral context is acknowledged, studies which have attempted to measure the constraint on letters have only used unilateral context. (Bilateral context occurs where there are words on both sides of the deletion; unilateral context where there are words on one side only – see Glossary). Using highly articulate subjects with language taken from both adult's and children's reading material, it has been shown that constraint does not increase uniformly with the length of context (Burton et al (1955), Carterette et al (1963)). Subjects were given parts of sentences of varying length which had the last letter missing. They were asked to supply the missing letter. Constraint increased most rapidly as the context increased from nought to three letters. After a context of nine letters very little increase in constraint was felt, and after 32 letters there was a virtual levelling off. In other words, the last letter of a sequence of 10,000 letters is no more predictable than the thirty-third one. Although this does not tell us much about word constraint, letter and word constraint are obviously interrelated to some degree. Constraint on single letters in a language sequence seems to reach a maximum somewhere between four and eight words, (32 letters).

Attempts to measure the effect of context length on word predictability have used Cloze Procedure. This is particularly useful because the results have a direct application to the preparation of passages for the classroom. Cloze Procedure takes two important factors into consideration which are missed from the letter studies. Each deletion will have a bilateral, as opposed to a unilateral context. The cumulative effects of deletions will be reflected in the results. Constraint *may* not increase after three words in a *sentence*, but if 40 sentences are put together with every fourth word missing, the constraint at the end of the passage may be seriously weakened by the removal of so many words earlier on. This constraint at the end *may* increase if only every sixth word is deleted.

Again, using highly articulate subjects, and deleting every second, third, fourth, fifth and sixth word from respective passages, Fillenbaum et al (1963) found that the greatest difference in constraint was between passages with every second and third word deleted respectively. There was little difference between passages which had every fourth, fifth or sixth words deleted. MacGinitie (1961) also found no statistically significant improvement in accuracy of prediction by subjects on passages which had deletions of every sixth, twelfth and twenty-fourth words. A more recent study by Alderson (1979) found that a bilateral context of up to ten words was the crucial amount of context that affected the ease of prediction. Above this amount of context the relationship with ease of prediction was not so consistent.

Figure VIII: Relationship between Length of Unilateral Context (in Letters) and Constraint

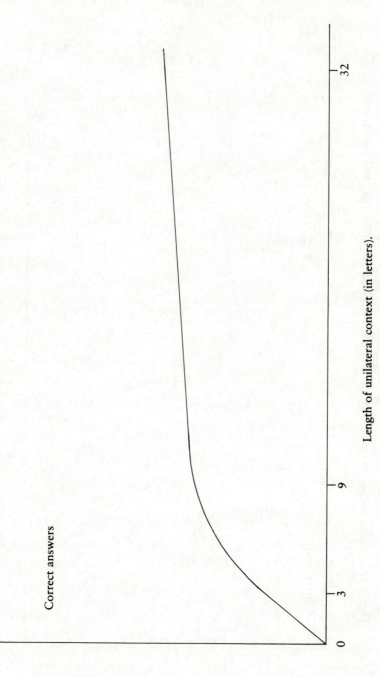

Correct answers

Length of unilateral context (in letters).

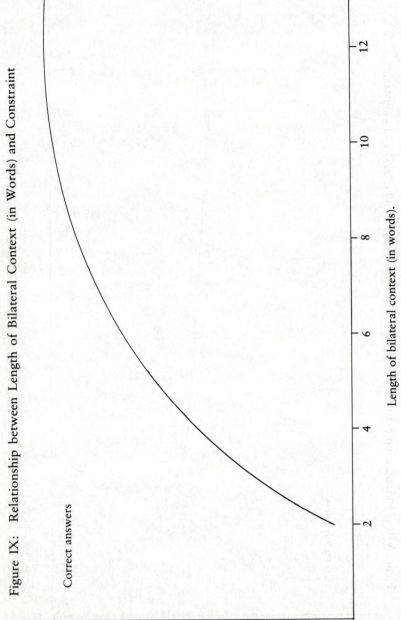

Figure IX: Relationship between Length of Bilateral Context (in Words) and Constraint

Correct answers

Length of bilateral context (in words).

It should be remembered that the exact amount of increase of constraint will vary from situation to situation. Although the increase would be great when moving from a two to a four word bilateral context, contexts which do not contain at least one noun, verb, adjective or adverb are not going to be important as those contexts which do. We cannot escape from the powerful influence of word class.

The subjects whom the teacher regularly faces are not highly articulate undergraduates. It would therefore seem that a bilateral context of about eight words ought to be regarded as a minimum when dealing with children. It would seem unwise to give less than this for more than the odd deletion unless, of course the teacher wished to stretch a particularly able group. Other than suggesting minimum figures it is pointless to hypothesize about the number of words where context reaches its maximum effect for children. The teacher must decide on the norm depending on the age and ability of the children concerned. However, I suspect that because of the way constraint is programmed into language, because of the limited memory span of the child, and because of the child's inability to make the most of the given context, the length for maximum effect for children will be very close to that of the length of adults. Provided the minimum context is supplied the teacher should be more concerned with the class and sentence position of possible deletions.

Practice

In Chapter Four we considered the importance of training pupils in group discussion and in how to exploit meaning by looking for contextual clues. Part of this training would involve pupils in doing passages which are easy at first, in order to ensure success, and which become progressively difficult. Even when pupils are competent in the procedure, the teacher still needs to be able to regulate the difficulty. Apart from there being some deletions which almost guarantee success, there also need to be deletions which will stimulate and stretch pupils. As pupils get used to a particular standard the teacher needs to be able to produce material of a slightly higher standard to encourage progress. Of equal importance is an understanding of why a task may be too difficult and an ability to regulate future material accordingly.

In an interesting study by Hepp (1979) it was found that pupils made most 'information gain' when they completed passages which had words of medium difficulty deleted. The relative difficulty of the words was defined in a technical, mathematical way. Hepp concluded that words which are of medium difficulty should be deleted when using cloze to develop comprehension. However, it must be remembered that Hepp's experimental groups were small (eighteen pupils), and it is a matter for debate as to whether or not comprehension in terms of 'information gain' is the same as comprehension in terms of 'an interrogation of the text'. Hepp also admits that the method of determining word difficulty in an exact mathematical way is too cumbersome to be taken seriously by most teachers. The guidelines given in this chapter, although less precise, are more likely to be of practical use. The value of this study is that it gives some empirical support to what some teachers have felt, namely that great care should be taken to ensure that the cloze deletions are demanding, but not too difficult or frustrating.

While it is not necessary to rigorously examine every deletion in the exact way that I have outlined below, the following are the kind of questions that need to be asked. Experience increases both skill and speed.

1. Is this passage suitable in terms of language difficulty and content?
2. Is the proposed deletion a structure or content word?
3. If it is a structure word, is it one that has been chosen deliberately in order to contribute to the ease of the task, or ought a content word be chosen?
4. If it is a content word, is it one which can reasonably be inferred, given the context and the pupils' general knowledge?
5. If it is a noun or a verb have too many been deleted from these classes already, thus making the overall task far to difficult?
6. Does the position of this proposed deletion make the task too difficult?
7. Does this proposed deletion have sufficient bilateral context?

By paying attention to deletion position and context length (especially in the early stages where it is more possible to vary these) and by paying particular attention to deletion class, I have tried to produce a passage which steadily increases the demands it makes on the reader.

Teacher Stress

What actually happens in the classroom is not ———— only major cause of stress in the professional life ———— teachers. This claim, which ———— in some ways surprising (although it appears more true ———— reflection), was made by two educationalists after ———— had conducted a random survey of two hundred and eighteen teachers ———— comprehensive schools. The results of their survey ———— analysis add further weight

——— the claims already being ——— about the unhappy state of the ———. Although there ——— exceptions, the general public have often ——— to appreciate the emotional and physical ——— that can be imposed ——— some classes on the best of ———. And, as this survey has ———, classroom stress ——— not the only ——— why some are discontented with their ———.

Stress is defined in the ——— as being a syndrome of ——— effects – an increase in the ——— rate, anger, depression ——— a perceived threat to ——— and well-being. This kind ——— syndrome can result in ——— low job satisfaction, ——— and a desire to ——— teaching. It is surely a ——— which all ——— the immediately successful have ——— at some stage in their career. ——— a quarter of those ——— filled in the ——— reported that they regarded ——— as either stressful or ——— stressful.

——— the many factors ——— work in the ——— such as pupil ——— were important, the ——— which were most ——— strongly associated with ——— satisfaction and the ——— to leave ——— were poor ——— structure and poor ———. It appears that ——— conditions are as ——— as the work ——— in contributing ——— teacher stress.

——— stress was reported by ——— teachers without ——— and by male ——— of Department. ——— teachers are also absent ——— than men. Teachers under thirty are more likely to leave the profession than their older colleagues.

(This passage was based on an article by C. Kyriacou and J. Sutcliffe printed in *Educational Research* 21, 2, 1979.)

Figure X Summary of Factors affecting Difficulty of Prediction

	Deletion Class	Deletion Position	Bilateral Context
	Structure	Middle	12
			11
			10
			9
DIFFICULTY		End	8
	Nouns Verbs		7
			6
	Adjectives Adverbs		5
		Beginning	4

It is difficult to increase complexity in a way which can be exactly measured and regulated. I have tried to produce a reasonably steady increase in difficulty over a few hundred words. This is the kind of progress that teachers need to aim at making over several thousand words, spread over many passages and many hours of conversation and thinking. The individual reader may have felt that the passage was too difficult towards the end. This difficulty would be reduced if the individual reader were to discuss the passage with a group of teacher readers who had some experience of cloze.

There are occasions when a teacher may wish to use Cloze Procedure for a purpose other than for general reading improvement. In these cases the teacher will need to choose the deletions according to a particular pattern (Chapter Two) or according to the specific requirements of the purpose. Examples of this latter practice are given in the next two chapters.

Summary

It is important to motivate the child to want to discuss a cloze passage by selecting a passage which is both interesting and not too difficult to read.

Structure words (such as conjunctions, articles, prepositions and auxiliary verbs) are easier to predict than *Content* words (nouns, main verbs, adjectives and adverbs). As a general rule, words in the middle of a sentence are easiest to predict; next easiest are words at the end of a sentence, and finally, words at the beginning of a sentence are the most difficult. Ease of prediction increases as context increases up to a bilateral context of ten words for adult readers.

Word class, deletion position, and the amount of context can all be regulated by the teacher to produce passages which are progressively demanding for the reader.

Chapter Six

Towards Diagnosis and Possible Remedies

Reading problems

It is one thing to know that a child has a reading problem and can only score a certain low mark on a reading test: it is an entirely different matter to know what is wrong with the child's reading ability, and to be able to help that child overcome specific problems. Edwards (1976) identified six main areas of reading failure:

i. *Insufficient Sight Vocabulary*. The child's fluency is hindered because the number of unknown words is too great.

ii. *Inadequate Visual Analysis Skills*. The child has difficulty in separating words into parts that are going to help in the recognition of words.

iii. *Inadequate Auditory Analysis Skills*. The child has difficulty in applying phonic analysis to both easy and difficult words.

iv. *Inability to use Context Clues*. The child has difficulty in using the information given in the text to anticipate the meaning of new and unfamiliar words.

v. *Inadequate Comprehension Skills*. The child has difficulty in gaining meaning from what is read and in thinking through the ideas in the text.

vi. *Inefficient Rates of Reading*. The child lacks the understanding of the need to adopt his reading style to suit his particular purpose for reading and the particular text being read.

Whilst general help with reading may be of value, it is likely to be of limited usefulness until specific problems have been diagnosed and specific help given.

Various diagnostic reading tests are available. These do not necessarily require the teacher to have special qualifications in order to administer them or interpret results. However, the diagnostic tests available to the ordinary teacher usually attempt diagnosis of problems in terms of a few broad categories. As such, they may provide a useful starting point for further investigation. Another way into diagnosis is for the teacher to talk to the child about any reading difficulty which may be experienced. Provided the child is reasonably intelligent, and provided meaningful records are kept, then this process may not be as fruitless as it may first appear. However, it is acknowledged that not all children will be able to articulate their problems, and there are likely to be problems that the children themselves will be unaware of.

Error Analysis

An important method for learning about a child's reading difficulties is to examine the mistakes that the child makes when reading. Being aware of the kind of errors that are being made is probably of more value than simply knowing the number of errors that are made. As Yetta Goodman (1972) has argued, *qualitative* rather than merely *quantitative* analysis is essential for diagnosis. In a study comparing the reading behaviour of dyslexics and normal readers, Thomson (1978) predicted that dyslexics would make more errors than normal readers. Not surprisingly this was the case. However, what was interesting and of most educational importance was that dyslexics tended to make completely different types of error to those made by normal readers. This enabled the author to draw important conclusions about the problems facing dyslexics when they read.

Errors in reading behaviour do not represent random substitutions. Each error has a cause, or series of causes. Errors represent an imperfect match between the print and the language generated by the reader. This mismatch between print and language production needs to be analysed carefully as this is where insight can be gained into the particular child's reading behaviour.

Various categories have been devised for recording and analysing errors that are made while a child reads a passage aloud to his teacher. Pumfrey (1976) gives an example of one of the simpler systems which classifies errors under the following headings:

Substitution
  The child reads 'the lady' instead of 'the woman'.
No response
  The child waits for help from the teacher before attempting the word.
Addition
  The child adds unprinted words to the sentence.

Omission
Self Correction
Repetition
Mispronunciation
Ignores punctuation
Reversals

    The child reads 'saw' instead of 'was', or 'no' instead of 'on'.

However, as Pumfrey points out, there are other systems for categorizing errors, that require considerable familiarity with linguistic concepts and are perhaps more suited to the psychologist's office than the classroom. Kenneth Goodman's taxonomy for the analysis of oral miscues comprises 28 categories.

Having recorded the errors that are made, the teacher then has to discover if there are any significant error patterns which emerge. Having noted the most common kind of error it is then necessary to hypothesize as to why these errors are being made. For example, using the categories given above, a high level of no-response errors would suggest an inadequate sight vocabulary and poor phonic ability.

Cloze Error Analysis

Reading requires pupils to utilize clues available in language, and, as has been argued, Cloze Procedure requires a similar ability. Written Cloze Procedure presents a more severe test than an oral reading of an unmutilated passage.

However, the teacher can be more confident that understanding is being measured as much as phonic ability. By analysing the errors made on cloze passages the teacher can gain an understanding of particular problem areas in the child's language production when reading. It has to be admitted that Cloze Procedure is likely to produce more errors than a child might make when reading an unmutilated version of the passage aloud to the teacher. This is due to the slightly unusual nature of the reading task. However, Cloze Procedure does reflect a deeper probing into the child's linguistic ability and can reveal areas of weakness that may go unnoticed by an analysis of oral miscues. One further advantage of Cloze Procedure over oral miscue analysis is that it more fully reflects the child's ability to use the total language context. The child can sit and reflect about meaning and can search the whole passage for clues. In reading aloud, all that is being demonstrated is the child's ability to use the most immediate clues, and possibly his or her ability to remember part of what has gone before. There is little opportunity for looking backwards or forwards in search of help. Finally, Cloze Procedure does have the advantage that it does not require a teacher to 'sit in' on the process. Cloze tests can be given to a whole class and analysed at the teacher's convenience. Cloze Procedure is a constructive language task and analysing errors shows weaknesses in that construction process.

In spite of the advantages of Cloze Procedure it must be admitted that oral miscue analysis can serve certain very useful functions. It is more useful than Cloze Procedure in diagnosing precise areas of inadequate sight vocabulary and of poor phonic ability. These errors would show up in a cloze test indirectly by there being a large number of errors because the child would have failed to process the print. The teacher would then need to listen to the child read in order to identify specific phonic problems.

Again, the cloze passages chosen should be ones which the children could be expected to cope with, and ones which they would find interesting enough to want to read. The more errors that the teacher has, the more confident he or she can be about their diagnosis. It is therefore necessary to diagnose errors that have been produced on several passages. Single passages which generate a high proportion of errors are likely to have been too difficult for the child and have therefore produced error data of dubious value.

A Proposed System For Cloze Error Categories

Meaningful diagnostic results cannot be obtained simply by analysing the errors according to the grammatical class of the deleted word. Although this may be a useful secondary procedure it is inadequate by itself. The word that is given by the pupil is of more value than the original word. In the following example the word in italics is the deleted word and the list of words underneath the sentence represents the errors that could have been made by different pupils.

The policeman saw the *men* lying by the roadside.
1. woman
2. man
3. she
4. mean
5. quickly
6. but
7. mans
8. donkey
9. rotten

These errors vary in the extent to which they reflect inadequate reading ability. For example, the errors in 3, 5 and 6 are arguably more serious than those in 1, 2, 7 and 8. Even here, depending on the wider context which is not given, it is arguable that the errors in 1 and 2 are less serious than those in 7 and 8. Again, 7 and 8 may represent different kinds of error. If all these errors had been recorded, simply in terms of a pupil failing to guess a noun correctly, the teacher would not be significantly further along the road to understanding what might be the child's problem. Examining what the child constructed is going to give us the clues.

Categories which allow very precise classification of every kind of error may be interesting and valuable for research purposes. However, diagnosis on such a level would probably be too daunting a task for most teachers. Such classification would yield too much information. Teachers need a system which will reveal general areas of concern in the first stage of diagnosis. Then, depending on the seriousness of the problem and the time available, one or more of these areas could be followed up as a second stage of diagnosis.

Stage one In the first stage of analysis, errors can be categorized under one of four headings. By having only four categories a degree of precision is inevitably lost and the teacher has to use his or her judgement in placing some errors which may not fall obviously into one category. However, these categories do provide a relatively simple means of helping to delineate problem areas. In the examples used incorrect responses are given in brackets after the deleted word which is italicized.

Type 1 Errors

Into this category come all errors which are semantically and syntactically acceptable. The errors make sense in the context of the whole passage and fit into the syntax of the sentence. In the majority of cases these errors will be synonyms or words which do not significantly alter the sense of the main meaning.

1. He didn't *look* (seem) seriously injured.
2. Can you imagine what the sergeant would *say* (do) when he read my report.
3. 'I was proceeding along Shambles Road when I came across a black, *dishevelled* (hairy) lump. . . .'

In the latter example the need for careful interpretation by the teacher can be seen. In the context of the passage 'hairy' is appropriate, even though it is a poor replacement for 'dishevelled'.

It should be noted that in one sense these responses are not 'errors' at all. If they had been produced in the context of discussion about a deletion the teacher would be able to give the reader credit for his or her response. Although 'correct answer' here is being taken to mean 'the original word given by the author', it is quite defensibly arguable that 'correct answer' is 'the word about whose appropriateness there is concensus among articulate, fluent and informed readers'. However, in that these words represent a failure by the pupils to match exactly the language produced by the author, they may provide information about the child's use of context, and therefore are to be recorded.

Type 2 Errors

Into this category come errors which are syntactically appropriate, but which are semantically inappropriate. They will usually be of the same class as the original word and acceptable in terms of tense, person, case and number.

1. I wasn't sure if *he* (you) could see or hear me.
2. I didn't know what to say to *him* (myself).
3. . . . take him to the nearest (largest) zoo.

In the context of the whole passage from which this error was taken 3 was judged to be semantically inappropriate.

The following error would not be syntactically acceptable in terms of Type 2 errors even though the original word and the error share the same word class. The incorrect verb form has been used.

4. He didn't *look* (looked) . . .

Type 3 Errors

Into this category come errors which are semantically acceptable and yet which are syntactically unacceptable. They will probably be words which share the same word stem as the missing word or have a similar meaning to it, and yet will be inappropriate in terms of tense, person, case and number. They may also be similar in meaning but be from a completely different word class.

1. The man had *fallen* (fell) into the rut.
2. He didn't *look* (looked, seems) seriously injured.
3. I came across a black, *dishevelled* (mess) lump.

Type 4 Errors

Into this category come responses which are totally unacceptable, either semantically or syntactically.

1. Green peas *were* (he) now racing round his intestines.

2. It's not *that* (was) we wanted.
3. 'I was proceeding *along* (a) Shambles Road . . .'

These four categories are an attempt to simplify the system used by Neville and Pugh (1974). At first sight they may still appear rather complicated. However, with practice teachers can soon become familiar with them.

Table VI shows some of the results that were obtained when a first stage analysis was carried out on the cloze errors of a group of thirteen-year-old backward readers. In the discussion which follows the pupils' names have been changed to help preserve anonymity. The number of errors that a child has in any one category has been expressed as a percentage of his or her total errors. This helps to identify pupils with similar or differing error patterns, regardless of the total number of errors made.

Table VI: First Stage Analysis of Cloze Errors

Name	Number Of Errors	Sem. √ Syn. √ Type 1	Sem. X Syn. √ Type 2	Sem. √ Syn. X Type 3	Sem. X Syn. X Type 4
Richard	31	16%	13%	19%	52%
Susan	22	4%	27%	9%	60%
Paul	22	26%	5%	10%	59%
Nigel	23	52%	13%	4%	30%
Steven	27	33%	11%	7%	48%
Ruth	20	30%	20%	5%	45%
Sally	28	36%	7%	7%	50%

Interpretation Part of the value of the procedure immediately becomes apparent when one examines the pattern of the sub-scores for children who made approximately the same number of errors. Simply by looking at the size of Type 1 and Type 4 errors the teacher can begin to gain an assessment of the seriousness of the reader's problem. The total number of errors would indicate that Richard was probably a poorer reader than Steven. Their relatively high proportion of Type 4 errors indicate that a large number of syntactic and semantic clues are being unused. One of Richard's problem areas appears to be his failure to be syntactically accurate. He has a far higher proportion of Type 3 errors than the rest of the group. Richard's relatively low proportion of Type 1 errors emphasizes the seriousness of his problem in comparison to Steven's.

Although Susan, Paul and Nigel share very similar scores, their error patterns are totally different. Of the three Nigel would appear to be the best reader and Susan the worst. Over half of Nigel's mistakes reveal a reasonable degree of accuracy in responding to the passage, and when compared with the other two, and with the whole group, he makes far fewer of the serious Type 4 errors. Although Susan and Paul make a similar number of Type 4 errors, Paul's Type 1 total is much higher than Susan's. This indicates a higher level of acceptably accurate responses. Susan's number of Type 2 errors suggests a good innate sense of grammatical sequence but very little attention being paid to meaning. In comparison to Nigel, Susan has made twice as many mistakes which were devoid of meaning in the context. Although her total number of errors is reasonably low she appears to lack strategies for working out the meaning of deletions which she finds difficult.

Type 1 Errors

These errors reveal that although the children have understood the passage on one level, and are familiar with the syntactical patterns of the passage, they have failed to make the precise linguistic match with the language of the writer. There may be at least three reasons for this.

  i. If the passage has a high proportion of uncommon words, these errors may either reflect the child's limited vocabulary, or the child's preference for common words.
      He *completed* (did) the task.
 ii. If the child has a sophisticated vocabulary he or she may be failing to appreciate information about the tone of the passage.
iii. These errors may represent the child's failure to use the clues available to deduce *precise* meaning. The right class of word is chosen and enough of the meaning is understood to enable the child to reject totally inappropriate words, but not sufficient is understood to produce the exact word.

Type 2 Errors

A comparatively high proportion of these would suggest that the children have a good appreciation of syntax, but that they are not understanding what they are reading. They can sense when a word from the wrong class has been produced in some cases, or when the wrong morphology has been used. However, they are probably focusing too much attention on the linguistic segment in question and ignoring the sense of the sentence and passage as a whole. They may be reading too fast. They may be too used to 'barking at print' without understanding meaning. If a high number of Type 2 errors is accompanied by a low number of Type 1 and Type 3 errors one could assume that the child needs to learn more about inferring meaning from existing information.

Type 3 Errors

Errors in this category represent two different problems. A child may suggest a word of the correct class and yet be inaccurate in the precise form of the word. Quite common failures with verbs are the suggestion of a word in the wrong tense, or in a form which does not agree with the number of the subject. On a more serious level a child may be able to understand the gist of what the writer is trying to say and yet fail to channel that understanding into the appropriate syntactic pattern of the context.

Type 4 Errors

These errors represent the most serious kind of failure because the children are not using either of the two main sources of help available to them. In order to help pupils with a high proportion of Type 4 errors, further individual diagnosis is necessary.

Stage Two Depending on the time available and the seriousness of the problem the teacher may wish to do a further analysis on the errors of some of his or her pupils. Clearly this would not be possible with every child on every occasion. The teacher's own previous knowledge of the child's language ability, his or her marking of the cloze scripts and the pattern of errors may together suggest need for improvement in a particular area. In Nigel's case it became apparent that the most obvious need was for vocabulary development.

If errors are to be examined in greater detail it must be remembered that too much detail can be counter-productive. The teacher needs to be selective if he or she and the pupils are not to be swamped with too much information to cope with. One example of a child's failure to generate a conjunction does not justify the suggestion that the child has difficulty with conjunctions. However, five or six such failures may suggest that a particular pattern is emerging. It is the patterns that are of interest. What is of value to the child is not the teacher's understanding of every error that has been made, but the teacher's ability to isolate one or perhaps two specific types of error and to devise teaching strategies to help improvement in these areas.

It may be felt that if a second stage analysis is to be carried out, the first stage is superfluous. What the first stage does is to help isolate the children with the most serious need, as well as giving some indication of the problem area. The first stage can provide useful hints about what to select for detailed inspection in the second stage. For example, if a child scored a high proportion of Type 3 errors the author would seek to find out why his or her grammatical sense was weak in a reanalysis of the errors.

In the second stage of analysis the teacher should look closely at each error in context and try to understand why the child has failed. The teacher needs to bear in mind two general questions.

Is there anything which the reader has ignored in producing this error?

Is there anything in the text which might explain how this error occurred?

The following is an extract from the notes the author made when taking a second look at Richard's errors.

Original Word	Error	Notes
more	hundred	... a few *more* (hundred) yards. Shows a limited understanding although the distance is unrealistic.
sight	it	... out of *sight* (it). Replaced noun with pronoun, but the 'it' is nowhere specified in context. Failure to use the sematic clues of previous sentence. '... round the corner' tells him that they couldn't be seen.
to	and	... for staying behind *to* (and) get the chocolate. Uses conjunction to create new phrase boundaries – staying behind, get the chocolate. Turned infinitive into command, but the tense of the new command is inconsistent with the rest of the passage. Change of tense from past to present.
were	he	(they) ... *were* (he) now racing round. Perhaps he has constructed a 'was' to produce – he was now racing round. His overall sentence makes no sense. He has no awareness of who the subject of the verb is. No awareness of the need to provide an auxilliary verb to meet the tense requirements.
quickly	to	... were being *quickly* (to) followed ... Possibly understood as – were being followed too/as well... If this is the case he clearly thinks that it is permissible to have the 'to' before the verb. It is a similar construction to the one above which is causing problems. Aux. Verb + Adverb + Main Verb.
had	just	... We *had* (just) started to run ... Wrong tense in the light of the whole passage, although 'just' makes sense if the immediate sentence it taken in isolation. Auxilliary verb replaced by adverb.

out	round	... coming *out* (round) of the school gate. He ignores the word after the deletion.
waiting	in	... We were *waiting* (in) nervously. He understands that they were waiting inside. Replaces verb with preposition.
being	look	... our parents were *being* (look) phoned ... Little use made of context at all. Main verb replaced by inappropriate verb. Failure to appreciate tense.
him	me	... I didn't know what to say to *him* (me). Wrong pronoun.
you	I	... Can *you* (I) imagine... Wrong pronoun.

It must be stressed that these are only a sample of the notes made and they are given as an example of how careful examination of cloze errors can reveal possible areas of weakness. They are not intended to 'prove a case', but merely to suggest possibilities. The first analysis indicated that Richard was particularly weak in the use of context clues and hinted at a poor sense of grammatical accuracy. The extract above tends to confirm these points. Although there are many problems one could pursue, two points in particular emerge which could be the subjects of a special teaching programme, apart from the general programme designed to improve his use of contextual information. First many of his errors centred around auxiliary verbs and main verbs. Particular attention needs to be drawn to tense and he needs to become more familiar with long verb phrases. Connected with this is the second area of confusion. He is often unsure about who the subject of the verb is. As well as needing practice in using pronouns he also needs practice in seeing a sentence as a whole and in understanding who or what is dominating it.

Possible Remedial Activities
The following methods for helping to improve certain aspects of reading are only part of the answer. They are given to emphasize the role that Cloze Procedure can play but the author certainly does not wish to argue that they are the only methods that should be used.

Problem: The child is able to understand the passage in one sense, but is unable to make sufficient inference to achieve a precise match with the language of the writer. There is also the possibility of a restricted vocabulary.
Possible Teaching Strategies
    i. Group cloze discussions. When the teacher goes over the passage with the class or group, it is essential that he or she

points out any context information which the pupils may have missed. If the pupils produce an inferior, but acceptable alternative, it is essential that the teacher explains why the author's word is better.

ii. Group cloze discussions with instructions for pupils to list as many words as they can for each deletion, possibly using a dictionary. Then, as usual, they have to give reasons for the choice of the final word.

Problem: The child is able to read with understanding and has a good vocabulary, but is relatively insensitive to the particular author's style or the tone of specific passage.

Possible Teaching Strategy

Group cloze discussion of carefully chosen deletions. The teacher should point out any clues to the style and tone of the passage.

Problem: The child has a reasonable sense of grammatical appropriateness but is weak at retaining meaning or in using it as a basis for inferences about further deletions.

Possible Teaching Strategy

Group cloze discussion of passages which have a selection of the key content words removed. In the early stages, and for longer with young or very poor readers, the teacher may need to be part of the discussion group in order to direct the children to the relevant context information and help them utilize it by skilful questioning.

Problem: The child is able to follow the gist of what is being conveyed in the passage but makes mistakes in substituting the wrong form of the correct word or synonym. For example he or she may give a plural noun when a singular is required, or a wrong verb tense.

Possible Teaching Strategy

Once the particular problem has been identified the teacher can construct cloze passages in which only problem words, or parts of problem words have been removed. Having explained to the child where mistakes are being made, this teaching can be backed up in the early stages with 'easy' part word deletions, followed by whole word deletions at a later stage. The part word deletions help give success to the child and also help focus attention on the problem area. The discussion of these passages is again ideally done in small groups.

For example, a child who had problems with verb forms could be given the following type of passage. (The same passage has been given with different deletion types to emphasize the progression.)

Passage A

Peter was sit – – – on the grass. Something suddenly dropp – – beside him. It w – – a note which had c – – – from over the fence.

Passage B

Peter was s——— on the grass. Something suddenly d——— beside him. It w——— a note which had c——— from over the fence.

Passage C

Peter was ——— on the grass. Something suddenly ——— beside him. It ——— a note which had ——— from over the fence.

If the deletions require the pupils to discuss a particular problem (in this case, verb endings), they are inevitably going to learn something about that problem through having to face it in cloze.

Problem: The child shows evidence of understanding the gist of the passage but fails to produce words of an acceptable grammatical class for the deletions. This reflects a more serious grammatical failure than the one outlined immediately above and suggests an unfamiliarity with certain grammatical patterns. The child's own speech grammar is almost certainly well developed, and he or she may know that their suggestions do not make sense. They simply cannot generate language according to the patterns of the text which is almost certainly more formal and sophisticated than their speech.

Possible Teaching Strategy

One way in which Cloze Procedure could help is to give the child passages which emphasize a particular problem area. If it is found that the child is having problems with phrases involving prepositions or adverbs for example, then he or she could be given passages which have certain of these types of words removed. Ideally this kind of exercise should be preceded by specific instruction and should be done as a group discussion exercise.

Problem: The child reveals an unawareness of phrase or sentence boundaries. This may reflect a failure to use punctuation to help when reading.

Susan screamed out at the teacher. *She* (angrily) ran out. It was all Robert's fault for staying behind *to* (and) get the chocolate.

In the first example the reader has ignored the full stop and tried to run two sentences together at the expense of the sense of the second one.

The idea of the girls screaming angrily is more important to the reader than the full stop. In the second example the reader has tried to create two disparate clauses by forcing a conjunction into a situation where it disrupts the flow of meaning.

Possible Teaching Strategy

Group cloze discussion of passages that have had words removed from the end of main units of meaning. In the early stages these deletions should be ones which are followed by clearly marked items of appropriate punctuation. Progression of difficulty can be achieved by gradually moving to the deletion of words from the beginning of main units of meaning. In this case the deletions should follow the appropriate punctuation.

One of the things which is most likely to destroy any interest in reading is the repeated demand by the teacher that pupils should complete hundreds of cloze passages by themselves in silence, which is what might happen if this chapter is misinterpreted. As has been argued throughout this book, Cloze Procedure can be a valuable activity but it needs to be introduced into the right environment, and the results which it yields need sensitive interpretation. This is especially so in the area of diagnosis.

Summary

If a teacher is to help children improve their reading ability in specific areas, he or she needs to try to understand what the specific reading problems facing the children are. One way of doing this is to examine the errors made on cloze passages. A relatively simple four category system was suggested for examining cloze errors in the first stage of analysis.

Type 1 Error	Grammar √
	Meaning √
Type 2 Error	Grammar √
	Meaning ×
Type 3 Error	Grammar ×
	Meaning √
Type 4 Error	Grammar ×
	Meaning ×

With a few children it may be possible to undertake a more thorough analysis by seeking to find out from the context why each error was made. From this second stage analysis understanding should be gained about the most common kinds of error the pupil is making.

The cloze group discussion exercise can be modified to help improve the pupils' ability to overcome specific difficulty. This will involve the teacher in constructing passages which delete the whole or part of words which are most likely to cause problems for the children concerned. Throughout all these exercises emphasis needs to be placed on teaching the children how to use context.

Chapter Seven

Cloze Across the Curriculum

Every Teacher is a Reading Teacher

It can no longer be assumed that the only teachers who have a professional responsibility for the teaching of reading are those in infant and junior schools, or those in remedial departments, with secondary English teachers having a nebulous role on the sidelines. Until quite recently books published on the teaching of reading were obviously aimed at teachers in the first three of the above four categories. However, it is wrong to think of reading as a particular skill that has been acquired by the age of eleven for 85 per cent of the population, needing only 'polishing up' in the secondary school. Reading involves thinking about meaning and as such is a process that needs continual development. As such, it is also a process that is crucial to learning across the whole of the curriculum. Reading is a tool for learning and therefore is encompassed by the professional responsibility of all teachers, regardless of their particular specialism in terms of subject or age of children taught. Reading about Viking raids or the digestive system is as much a part of doing history or biology as is listening to a teacher talk about the same subjects. Just as certain activities associated with writing and talking have been recognized as being of tremendous value in helping children to assimilate and develop new ideas, so too reading can no longer be seen as having a restricted domain in schools. Learning a subject involves using language in relation to that subject, and reading is an important language activity. Perhaps the greatest loss to meaningful education since the Bullock Report has not been the insistent whittling away of money but the failure of most teachers with responsibility for curriculum development to effectively implement the following recommendations:

3. Every school should devise a systematic policy for the development of reading competence in pupils of all ages and ability levels.

4. Every school should have an organized policy for language across the curriculum, establishing every teacher's involvement and reading competence in pupils of all ages and ability levels.

5. Every school should have a qualified teacher with responsibility for advising and supporting his colleagues in language and the teaching of reading. (p. 514 op. cit.)

Everything which has been said in previous chapters concerning the development of general reading competence is obviously relevant to reading for learning in the subject areas. Cloze Procedure is particularly useful for the subject specialist in two ways: it is helpful as a means of assessing understanding of a subject and it is also a useful means of encouraging pupils to develop their knowledge of a subject.

Assessing Subject Knowledge

In passages of prose which do not have vast amounts of subject-specific knowledge, one could reasonably expect most children to have some understanding of the content. They would be able to make inferences about deletions based on their experience of life and general knowledge, as well as on contextual information. If the following sentences were taken from a story the reader would not need specialized knowledge to guess the deleted word.

The conductor rang the bell, telling the driver to pull up at the next stop. Three ladies got off before the ———— drove away.

It could be safely assumed that most readers would bring enough general knowledge with them to enable them to infer the word 'bus'.

However, passages in many school books contain meaning that is not simply 'common sense' to most child readers when they come to them for the first time. In many instances they are being directed to the texts to get information from them. A reader of this book should have learned enough to make a reasonable attempt at filling in deletions in the following passage.

Cloze Procedure involves the ———— of words from passages of ————. Readers are then expected to make suggestions as to what the ———— words are. They can discuss together and try to select the best word – the word which they think the ———— would have used. Readers need to be taught how to use ———— and ———— information given in the text. The name for the procedure is derived from a term used by ———— psychologists.

However, imagine such a passage being presented to you before an understanding of Cloze Procedure had become part of the knowledge that you would bring to the passage.

Because knowledge of a subject is necessary before detailed

discussion can be held about that subject, it is not advisable to use Cloze Procedure as a means of introducing a new topic. However, it can be used to test how much a child already knows about a topic, and as will be argued later, it is extremely useful as a means of revising concepts that have already been introduced.

Look carefully at the following two passages of biology. Which one most effectively tests biological knowledge?

Passage A

Flower Structure: The Wallflower
The flower is the ——— of the plant that ——— the reproductive structures. In ——— wallflower, male and female ——— present in the same ———.

Passage B

Flower Structure: The Wallflower
The ——— is the part of the ——— that holds the ——— structures. In the wallflower, ——— and female are present in the ——— flower.

As has been seen, cloze tests are valid and reliable measures of how far a reader is able to predict the language sequence of a text. When parts of the main content of the text are removed, namely when certain nouns and verbs are deleted, the resulting test can be used to assess the reader's understanding of the content of the text. Although all cloze tests inevitably assess an understanding of content, the removal of only certain content words frees the reader from having to concentrate on syntax and puts a greater emphasis on the 'actors' and their states, processes and actions. Passage B is a more effective test of biological knowledge than Passage A. The deleted words from Passage B are more subject-specific than those from Passage A.

Passage A	*Passage B*
part	flower
holds	plant
the	reproductive
are	male
flower	same

In 1957 Taylor gave a series of cloze tests and comprehension tests to American Air Force Trainees to test their understanding of a technical article of the American Air Force system of supply. In this study three homogeneous groups were given different types of cloze test. The *Any* test was a passage with any class of word deleted on a numerical basis; the *Easy* test had only conjunctions, prepositions, articles, pronouns and verb auxiliaries removed; the *Hard* test had certain nouns, verbs and adverbs removed. Before reading the technical article the trainees were given a comprehension test on its content. They were also given a cloze test on the article. A week or so later they were given the article to read, followed by an immediate recall comprehension test and a cloze test. The following is a summary of Taylor's results.

Table VII: Mean Scores on Cloze and Comprehesion Tests

Cloze Group (N)	Cloze Tests		Comprehension Tests	
	Before Reading	After Reading	Before Reading	After Reading
Any (48)	22.8	31.3	26.2	31.0
Easy (52)	39.8	44.8	25.2	32.4
Hard (52)	19.1	27.6	26.2	33.1

As was anticipated, the removal of content words did make that particular test the most difficult cloze test. However, it was this cloze test which produced the highest correlations with the scores on the comprehension tests designed to assess the subjects' understanding of the technical article.

Table VIII: Correlation between Score on the Cloze and Comprehension Tests

	Any	Easy	Hard
Before cloze v Before comprehension	.70	.58	.92
After cloze v After comprehension	.80	.64	.80

Considering all the information available to him Taylor considered the *Any* test to be the one which is most useful overall, which is why he recommends it for general readability purposes. However, the *Hard* test did prove to be as valuable as the *Any* test in assessing understanding of content after the reading of the article, and it proved to be more useful than the *Any* when it came to assessing the prior knowledge of the content of the article that the reader had.

By squaring a product moment correlation coefficient one can calculate the maximum percentage of variance on one test that can be explained by the variance on the other test. In other words, a squared product moment correlation coefficient enables us to estimate how much overlap there is between the two tests. It enables us to see how far both tests are measuring the same thing. The value of Taylor's *Hard* cloze test correlation with the Before Reading Comprehension test can now be better appreciated. There was an estimated 85 per cent ($.92^2$) overlap between the two tests. (See Figure XI)

Figure XI: The Percentage of Variance in Taylor's Comprehension Test that can be predicted by the Cloze Test

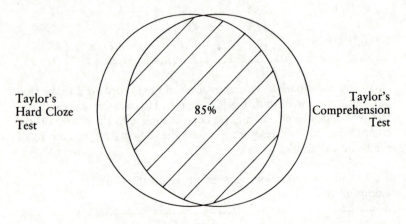

Taylor's
Hard Cloze
Test
85%
Taylor's
Comprehension
Test

If a teacher wishes to assess a class's previous experience of the concepts and vocabulary of a topic before a course of instruction, the assessment could be achieved by constructing a *Hard* cloze test. In Taylor's test he aimed at deleting every tenth word. However, if the tenth word was not a noun, verb or adverb he chose the nearest suitable to the tenth one. Alternatively teachers may not wish to stick too rigidly to Taylor's quasi-numerical deletion system and may prefer to select certain key words for deletion. If the latter practice is adopted, care should be taken to ensure that the passage is not made impossibly difficult by the deletion of too many key concepts.

In the following passage on the wallflower several key terms have been deleted to test the reader's biological knowledge. The deleted words have been supplied in italics for the reader's convenience.

Flower Structure: The Wallflower
The *flower* is the part of the plant that holds the *reproductive* structures. In the wallflower, male and female are present in the *same* flower.

The four *sepals*, called collectively the *calyx*, are small green or reddish structures. They *protect* the rest of the flower in bud and fold back as the flower opens.

The *four* petals, called collectively the *corolla*, are brightly coloured and *scented*. Insects are attracted to the flower by the colour, the scent, the *nectar* (a sugary liquid), and the *pollen*.

The six *stamens*, called collectively the androecium, are the *male* part of the plant. Each stamen is a filament with four pollen sacs (called the *anther*). The pollen grains contain the male *gametes* or reproductive cells.

The *female* parts are called the *gynaeceum*. The gynaeceum of the wallflower consists of an ovary, a *style* and a stigma. The *stigma* has a rough surface so that pollen grains which fall on to it will stick to it.

Such a test would obviously be extremely difficult for a person with no knowledge of the subject in question. However, if the same test were given after the reader had been given a course of instruction in the structure of the wallflower, the test would be an extremely useful indicator as to how far the reader had understood the essential vocabulary and concepts of the subject.

Apart from being useful in assessing the knowledge a reader may have before or after a course of instruction, cloze passages can be extremely useful in helping pupils discuss the subject. Through discussion they are making the concepts and vocabulary their own. They can use their peers as sounding boards and can iron out problems of understanding, as well as become more confident in handling their newly acquired knowledge.

Subject Discussion
The passage on the wallflower which I have argued could be used as a test, could also be used as a basis for group discussion. Such an exercise would obviously help the group to revise their understanding of the new topic and use vocabulary which may seem strange to them until they are encouraged to use the terms themselves. The guidelines given in Chapter Four concerning the group size and group training in cloze would need to be followed. However, there is no reason why Cloze Procedure should not be used in any subject area to promote discussion about a subject, and encourage pupils to understand and use the language of that subject, thus learning to read in that subject

and learn about that subject. The remainder of the chapter looks at how Cloze Procedure could be used to promote discussion in other areas of the curriculum. The fact that the author draws examples from only three areas does not preclude the use of the technique in other subjects.

Languages One would expect Cloze Procedure to be a valid means of assessing how far the language patterns of a subject agree with the language patterns of a writer, *regardless* of the particular language being used. Cloze Procedure is a sampling procedure, and because all languages have grammatical and semantic constraints inherent in them, the usefulness of Cloze Procedure is not restricted to a particular language. Various studies have used Cloze Procedure on many languages. A recent one by Landsheere (1972) confirmed all of Taylor's major findings using Cloze Procedure on the French language, and there appears to be no reason why the same should not be true with other languages.

There is a growing body of literature which indicates the usefulness of Cloze Procedure in the teaching of English as a Foreign Language. Gefen (1979) reports that the Procedure is regarded with such confidence in Israel that a Cloze Test is now included in the Israeli Matriculation Examination in English. The test has been well received by teachers who are reportedly developing their own cloze exercises to extend written and oral comprehension ability, and to test their pupils' appreciation of English grammar and vocabulary.

It is not too difficult to see how these same methods could be applied to the teaching of other languages. First, Cloze Procedure could be used as outlined in Chapter Three to get a comparative assessment of pupils' reading ability in the language in question. Secondly, it could be used to test an understanding of specific language points. Say, for example, that one wished to teach the pupils the necessary phrases to enable them to go into a French post office and buy a stamp. One could teach the necessary vocabulary and test it, not by giving the traditional vocabulary test, but by using a cloze passage with specific words deleted. A suitable French passage could be written by the teacher – in this particular case a hypothetical dialogue might be used. Certain key content words are deleted. The precise difficulty of the passage is determined by the teacher. By this method it may be that not every item of vocabulary is tested, and that the test may be less severe than a traditional one. However, the test is much more meaningful because the pupil is being expected to generate and use language in a quasi-realistic context. This kind of exercise could also be done in small groups and be used as a means of revision rather than as a test.

One useful way of developing understanding and discussion about a language is to use cloze passages as a basis for discussion in groups, as outlined in Chapter Four. The following passage was taken from a popular first-year French book. For the reader's convenience, words to be deleted have again been printed in italics rather than removed.

Les Marsaud sont en vacances au bord de la mer. On *voit* leur tente près de *la* plage. M. et Mme. Marsaud sont *assis* devant le café du *camping*. Ils regardent la plage *où* les enfants jouent. Jean-Paul et Claudette *jouent* au volley-ball avec *leurs* amis. Marie-France ne joue pas *au* volley-ball. Elle s'assied sur la *plage*. Bientôt son amie Monique *arrive*.
(Adapted from p. 129, S. Moore and A.L. Antrobus, *Longmans Audio Visual French, Stage A1*.)

Provided that the children are trained how to use context and are given instructions to provide a reason for their choice of word, this relatively simple passage could stimulate discussion about the following.

  i. The use of the verb 'voir' in the expression 'on voit'.
  ii. The gender of 'plage'.
  iii. Agreement of past participle and subject – 'assis'.
  iv. Vocabulary – le café du camping, la plage, arriver, s'assoir.
  v. Conjunctions – 'où'.
  vi. Agreement of adjective and subject – 'leurs'.
  vii. Contractions – 'au'.
  viii. Agreement of subject and verb – 'arrive'.

With groups of able pupils the teacher could insist that the group hold the discussion in the language in question, as far as possible. At first this is bound to hinder the important practice of giving reasons for choosing a word. However, this reluctance to speak may soon disappear, particularly in the context of a small group. This kind of exercise would seem ideally suited for language assistants to use with sixth formers.

Humanities Provided that the pupils have already been introduced to the topic in question, Cloze Procedure can be used across the whole curriculum to stimulate a discussion. Below is a passage that was given to three thirteen-year-old girls from the top stream in a secondary modern school. It was given to them as a geography revision exercise. Life in an Ibo village had been covered as a topic in the week prior to the discussion. The passage could have been given to them as a test to see how much they had remembered. In this instance it was given to them as a means of helping them reinforce what they already knew by getting them to use some of the concepts they had already acquired about Ibo village life. When reading the passage note that many of the words which have been deleted are reasonably specific to the subject in the sense that many of them would not be common knowledge to the pupils before coming to geography lessons. Again the deleted words have been given in italics for the reader's convenience.

An Ibo Village

Read the following passage carefully. Certain words have been missed out, one word from each space. Try to work out what each missing word is. It is very important that you discuss your reasons for choosing each word with other members of the group.

Almost every man in the village is a farmer, depending for food on the crops he can grow for his family. Root crops can grow quickly and easily due to the *heavy* rain and the long *wet* season. *Yams*, rather like large potatoes, are the main crop of most farmers. *Cassava*, a similar plant, which in Britain we eat as tapioca, is another crop grown by many villages. To plant either of these the farmer must clear away all the undergrowth of small bushes and weeds. This covers land which he may not have used for a year or two. He will *burn* the heaps of undergrowth in January or February. The ashes contain *chemicals* which help the plants to grow, so he spreads the *ashes* over the ground.

A farmer owns about two *hectares* of land but this is divided into *many* small, scattered plots, perhaps fifteen or twenty of them; some are near his home, others two or three kilometres away. When some of these plots have been cleared, the men and often the *women* also scrape at the surface with short-handled *hoes*, or digging sticks, to build the earth up into small mounds. In the top of each *mound* a small *yam* is planted and along the sides, other crops such as beans and green *vegetables*.

While the crops are growing the Ibo villagers live on food stored from the previous year's harvest. This is mainly *flour* made by grinding *yams* or cassava. The sale of *palm* oil and occasionally some *vegetables* and yams may earn a farmer about £25 a year. With this he pays *taxes* to the government, buys cloth and maybe a few tools, pots and baskets.

Despite such a small income a farmer seldom cultivates more than half his land in any year; the other half he leaves *fallow* – uncultivated, without any crops – so that the soil does not become exhausted. By doing this the soil slowly regains its *fertility* as new humus is formed from the *decaying* of falling leaves.

(Adapted from *Patterns in Geography, Book Two*, pp. 42–3, W. Farleigh Rice, Longman.)

The transcript which is given below gives extracts of the conversation which these three girls had. As you read the transcript note the way in which the girls reveal their understanding of the concepts involved and in fact are doing a fair bit of 'geography revision' as they talk together.

Elizabeth:	Something rather like . . . yams. This is . . .
Susan:	Yes, yams. They've got a lot of *them*.

Carol:	Yes yams. They're root crops.
Elizabeth:	That's what they eat.
Susan:	They're like potatoes. Potatoes in't crops.
Elizabeth:	Yes, because they're like large, long potatoes.
Susan:	Yams . . . they're horrible.
Carol:	They're horrible.
Elizabeth:	Well, they're meant to be like potatoes. They've got to be yams.
Carol:	Hum . . .
Elizabeth:	And they eat them so . . .
Carol:	They eat a lot of them. They're easy to grow. They're root crops, so it *must* be them.
Elizabeth:	Yams, rather like large, long potatoes, are the main crop of most farmers. Something, a similar plant which in Britain we eat as tapioca . . .
Susan:	That's cassava.
Elizabeth:	Why? How do you know?
Susan:	'Cos I read it in the book. (Laughter.)
Carol:	'Cos that's like rice.
Elizabeth:	A similar plant which we eat in Britain . . . we eat . . .
Susan:	Well I don't eat it!
Carol:	I do. Frogs' Spawn!
Elizabeth:	We've got to give a reason why.
Susan:	'Cos it said it in the book.
Carol:	That's the same as tapioca.
Susan:	Yes.

*****

Elizabeth:	He will something heaps of ground in January or February . . .
Susan:	Burn.
Carol:	Fertilize them.
Elizabeth:	No, it says the ashes contain something.
Carol:	Yes, it's burn.
Susan:	It's burn them 'cos the ashes.
Carol:	Yes, they'd burn to destroy all the shrubs and that.
Susan:	It must be burn to get the ashes.
Carol:	They'd burn to get all the weeds and everything out.
Susan:	Yes.
Elizabeth:	Yes, burn to make the ashes.
Susan:	Yes, burn.

Elizabeth:	Yes, burn to make the ashes.
Susan:	For fertilizer.
Elizabeth:	Yes, to spread over the ground for fertilizer.
Carol:	Yes.

*****

Elizabeth:	The ashes contain what?
Susan:	Chemicals.
Carol:	Yes, that's chemicals.
Elizabeth:	The ashes contain chemicals which ... Why chemicals? How do you know it's chemicals?
Carol:	'Cos the ashes ... 'cos there's chemicals ... 'cos there's chemicals in the plant in't there.
Elizabeth:	Yes, there's chemicals in the ashes.
Susan:	There's chemicals in the plant.
Elizabeth:	So he spreads the what? The ashes contain chemicals so he spreads the something over the ground.
Susan:	Ashes.
Elizabeth:	Yes, all right.

******

Elizabeth:	When some of the plots have been cleared the men and often the something also ...
Carol:	Women.
Susan:	Yes.
Elizabeth:	But we've got to give a reason why women do it.
Carol:	'Cos they do work as well.
Susan:	'Cos they help.
Carol:	Yes. They have to don't they.
Elizabeth:	Everyone's got to help to get the food.
Susan:	If they don't help they get no food.

*****

Elizabeth:	This is mainly something made by grinding something or cassava.
Susan:	Flour.
Carol:	You what?
Susan:	Flour, 'cos they grind up yams to make flour.
Elizabeth:	This is mainly ...
Carol:	Yes, but it can't be yams. They grind up cassava stuff.
Susan:	Yes, but they grind up yams as well.

Elizabeth:	This is mainly flour . . .
Carol:	Cassava 'cos . . .
Elizabeth:	'Cos when they grind the yams down they use it as flour.
Carol:	You can't grind yams into powder.
Elizabeth:	You do. They're like potatoes. They grind potatoes up don't they. How do you think they get *Wondermash*. (Laughter.) Yes, they take water out of it. This is mainly flour made by grinding . . .
Susan:	Yams or cassava.
Elizabeth:	Yams.
Susan:	They grow those.
Elizabeth:	It's got to be. Yams can be ground to flour.

Although I hope this transcript speaks for itself, I would like to repeat a point which is so crucial to Cloze Procedure before leaving it. The success of this conversation has largely been determined by the insistence of one member that a reason be given for every word chosen.

Literature Cloze Procedure has a particular application to the teaching of literature, although it must be admitted that it is only likely to be effective with certain groups, namely able pupils and adults.

In Chapter One it was suggested that a modified form of Cloze Procedure could be used to help pupils appreciate why an author or poet may have chosen a particular word. Words are deleted and then given in a list at the end of the passage. This exercise becomes much more demanding and interesting if the deleted words are not given. Groups can then discuss these deletions and judge the suggested words against two sets of criteria. The first set is the set which is applicable to all deletions, namely semantic and syntactic constraints. The second set of criteria involves an understanding of the kind of arguments that are made in certain aspects of literary criticism. If the groups are given training in the kind of 'literary argument' that can be brought into play, in addition to semantic and syntactic ones, then groups may find themselves searching the text very closely. This will almost inevitably lead to a better appreciation of the text and a growing confidence in the use of 'literary argument'.

Although the following list is not meant to be exhaustive by any means, it does illustrate some of the points which could be raised by a group in addition to obvious points about grammar and meaning.

i. Is the sound of the word related to the meaning the author wishes to convey?

    ii. Does the word fit into any metre or rhyme scheme?

   iii. Does the suggested word have any unfortunate or helpful connotations in the context of the passage?

   iv. Does the suggested word fit into any pattern of imagery that is being used?

   v. Is the suggested word 'echoed' earlier or later in the poem or extract?

   vi. How appropriate is the suggested word in the light of general knowledge about the author's style, or the style used in this particular work or passage?

In the extract from Wilfred Owen's poem *Anthem for Doomed Youth* given below, it is possible to find several words which would be semantically and syntactically appropriate for the deletion, and yet which from a literary point of view would be far less appropriate than Owen's word.

> What passing-bells for these who die as cattle?
> Only the monstrous anger of the guns.
> Only the ———— rifles' rapid rattle
> Can patter out their hasty orisons.

Discussion about appropriate alternatives is likely to lead an able group into an awareness of the strength of feeling in these lines, the irony, the use of onomatopoeia. After the correct word has been chosen or the answer given the ground has been prepared for an appreciation of why Owen used 'stuttering' in this context. In the light of an awareness of which word was actually used the group could then search the context again to see what clues are given which make this word particularly appropriate.

Summary

It has been argued that all teachers have a responsibility to encourage reading development. Cloze Procedure is just one way of encouraging pupils to read for meaning in all subjects.

    Cloze passages which have certain content words removed can be used to give indication of how far a pupil has understood the subject of the passage. However, such passages are also a useful means of encouraging discussion about the subject. They give the pupils opportunity to use newly acquired knowledge and thus help the pupils to make sense of that knowledge in their own terms. Although examples were drawn from the teaching of biology, French, geography and literature, there appears to be no reason why cloze passages should not be used across the whole curriculum.

Appendix

A Statistical Test for Evaluating the Difference Between Two Sets of Scores Obtained from the Same Group of People.
A use for this test would be to evaluate the difference between the cloze readability scores obtained from one book with those obtained from another book by the same group.

For a full treatment of the significance of difference between scores, the reader is referred to Lewis (1973) or Guilford et al (1978). It must be stressed that all statistical tests make assumptions and that it is a matter for judgement as to how far these assumptions are justified in any particular case. It must also be stressed that results obtained from a group of less than thirty children should be interpreted with caution. In the example below only ten pairs of scores have been used, for convenience.

In the following test it is being assumed that:

    i. The underlying population distribution is normal.
    ii. The samples have approximately equal variances.

If the reader does not understand these assumptions, he or she is *strongly advised* to consult one of the books mentioned above before applying the test.

Test for correlated samples 1. If the maximum possible score was the same on both tests then the results can be compared without further treatment. If the maximum possible scores were different for the two tests it is first necessary to express each score as a percentage score.

$$\text{Percentage Score} = \frac{\text{Obtained Score}}{\text{Maximum Possible Score}} \times 100$$

2. List the scores, (or the percentage scores if appropriate), that each child obtained on the two tests. Find the difference between the two scores for each child.

Child	Test 1	Test 2		d
A	5	6	6–5 =	1
B	4	3	3–4 =	–1
C	2	5	5–2 =	3
D	3	7	7–3 =	4
E	3	8	8–3 =	5
F	5	6	6–5 =	1
G	6	5	5–6 =	–1
H	7	9	9–7 =	2
I	6	10	10–6 =	4
J	8	10	10–8 =	2
			Sd =	20

The difference d = Score 2 − Score 1.

3. Find the sum of the difference scores by adding them together. In this case Sd = 20

4. Find the mean of the difference scores by dividing their sum by the number of pupils.

$$Md = Sd/N$$

In this case

$$Md = 20/10 = 2$$

5. Find the deviation of each difference score from the mean of the difference scores. Do this by subtracting the mean of the difference scores from each difference score.

$$xd = d - Md$$

6. Square the value of each xd.

Child	Test 1	Test 2	d		(d–Md) xd	x^2d
A	5	6	1	1–2 =	–1	1
B	4	3	–1	–1–2 =	–3	9
C	2	5	3	3–2 =	1	1
D	3	7	4	4–2 =	2	4
E	3	8	5	5–2 =	3	9
F	5	6	1	1–2 =	–1	1
G	6	5	–1	–1–2 =	–3	9
H	7	9	2	2–2 =	0	0
I	6	10	4	4–2 =	2	4
J	8	10	2	2–2 =	0	0
					$Sx^2d =$	38